Storage

1

158.2
GREENWALD

Greenwald, Jerry A
  Creative intimacy : how to break
the patterns that poison your relationships / by Jerry A. Greenwald. -- New York : Simon and Schuster, c1975.
  202 p. ; 22 cm.

ISBN 0-671-22160-4

  1. Intimacy (Psychology) 2.
Gestalt therapy. I. Title.

BF575.I5G73   158'.2

                                        75-25821
                                           MARC
Library of Congress
3767   529998   © THE BAKER & TAYLOR CO.   6078

CREATIVE INTIMACY

HOW TO BREAK THE PATTERNS THAT POISON YOUR RELATIONSHIPS

BY

Dr. JERRY A. GREENWALD

SIMON AND SCHUSTER
NEW YORK

Designed by Irving Perkins
Manufactured in the United States of America

1   2   3   4   5   6   7   8   9   10

Library of Congress Cataloging in Publication Data

Greenwald, Jerry A.
    Creative intimacy.
    1. Intimacy (Psychology)   2. Gestalt therapy.
I. Title.
BF575.15G73   158'.2   75-25821
ISBN 0-671-22160-4

1

To Tela

CONTENTS

FOREWORD   9
PREFACE   11

PART ONE
WHAT IS CREATIVE INTIMACY?

1. WHAT IS CREATIVE INTIMACY?   17
2. THE STRUCTURE OF AN INTIMACY OF TWO   29
3. THE INTIMATE SELF   36
4. ONE-TO-ONE INTIMACY   64

PART TWO
TOXIC PATTERNS AND TOXIC MYTHS

5. TOXIC PATTERNS IN INTIMATE RELATING   85
   Toxic Pairing   85
   Toxic Avoidance   88
   Toxic "Helpfulness"   96
   Toxic Projection   99
   Toxic Games   104
   Toxic Isolation   110
6. TOXIC MYTHS ABOUT INTIMACY   114
7. MULTIPLE RELATIONSHIPS: THE AVOIDANCE
   OF INTIMACY   131

PART THREE
ANTIDOTES

8. Awareness, Communication and
   Confrontation   145
9. Toxic Freedom (You only live once so take
   all you can get) and Its Antidote   160
10. The Poison of Permissiveness . . . and
    Its Antidote   165
11. Violations of Psychic Space . . . and
    Their Antidotes   169
12. Toxic Attitudes Toward Insecurity . . .
    and Their Antidote   173
13. Toxic Conflict in Intimacy . . . and
    Its Antidote   176
14. The Basic Attitude in Seeking Antidotes:
    "This Is Me"   178

PART FOUR
FINDING, NOURISHING AND—SOMETIMES—SAYING GOODBYE TO YOUR INTIMATE OTHER

15. How to Find an Intimate Other   183
16. It Takes Time to Love   186
17. Now Is Always the Beginning   191

FOREWORD

This book attempts to define the nature and meaning of intimate relationships between two adults and to outline the nourishing ways of relating that lead to the development and sustenance of such relationships. Equal attention is given to the toxic behavior patterns with which we poison existing intimate relationships or abort their development. Antidotes to these toxic patterns are also explored.

Creative Intimacy examines in more detail some aspects of my previous book, *Be the Person You Were Meant to Be*. Written within the framework of the philosophy of Gestalt therapy, *Creative Intimacy* continues to emphasize *awareness* of nourishing and toxic attitudes and behavior patterns and how these affect our relationships with others in the here and now.

PREFACE

The more impersonal our society and its institutions become, the more the individual feels alone, alienated and lost. He then lives in a chronically toxic condition. The person adrift in the world with no anchor loses his identity, the meaningfulness of his life and, eventually, his emotional and physical health. The most vital *and* most effective source of security and emotional nourishment is available within ourselves. Discovering and developing this inner strength is the primary antidote to our fears of loneliness and alienation.

This inner fortress of strength and security is built of self-love and self-acceptance and is based on the discovery and nourishment of our identities within ourselves *and within our intimate relationships*. In this increasingly impersonal world it is a matter of self-preservation that we learn how to establish, protect and maintain our personal psychic space—the areas that we know are important to ourselves and to others, especially to our Intimate Other.

Without this fortress it is impossible to protect and nourish those vulnerable qualities that enable us to relate to others as loving, caring human beings. Building our fortress is a two-step process. First, we need to discover how to relate intimately with ourselves; and second, we need to discover how to relate intimately with an Intimate Other, a relationship I call an Intimacy of Two.

This process requires a degree of awareness and creative adjustment to the changing realities of the world. If we expect the same responsiveness from a modern bureaucracy which we might have found in a town meeting, we are poisoning ourselves with an attitude that is obsolete in the reality of the now. Similarly, intimate relating is a changing process, not a fixed state. Real intimacy with oneself is the most powerful antidote against the forces that threaten to mechanize and dehumanize us all. It also provides the most reliable foundation for other love relationships, including the love of humankind.

The ultimate in human interaction is intimate one-to-one relating. Only here does there exist the potential for experiencing the full richness possible in human relating. The need for intimate relationships is deeply rooted in human nature and will never be obsolete. Yet many people today have been led to believe that the concept of an enduring intimate relationship with one other person is an obsolete notion. This tragedy is the result of false notions and ignorance about intimate relating—about what it is, how to discover it and how to nourish it.

The enormous effort required in the past for sheer survival has been cut to a fraction, making available time and energy that, if used creatively, can be an incomparable boon toward discovering and experiencing a more meaningful life. However, if unused or misused, this energy produces the toxic effects we experience as tension, anxiety or restlessness and can ultimately lead to destructive behavior toward ourselves and others. For example, although people have more time than ever to discover and explore the richness of an Intimacy of Two, many tend to become so excessively preoccupied with "successful" relating that it becomes an obsession. As essential as intimate relationships may be to our well-being they represent only one area of the emotional needs of the whole person. Therefore, when the importance of these relationships is blown out of proportion, they have a toxic effect in that they blind us to the variety and depth of human experiences available in many other areas of living. Too much of anything—however nourishing—becomes toxic.

We risk the loss of our own existence when we become preoccupied with relationships with others *at the expense of achieving intimacy within ourselves*. Only through inner intimacy can we gain full appreciation of the endless dimensions and depth of experiencing our total selves and all that exists within our world.

Many of us poison ourselves with the illusions that beauty, success, sexual know-how or the application of modern psychological techniques provides the key to intimate relationships. We take a giant step toward true intimacy when we recognize that intimate relating is a self-initiated, self-sustaining process requiring a continuing interest and a willingness to work at it.

PART ONE

WHAT IS CREATIVE INTIMACY?

1

WHAT IS CREATIVE INTIMACY?

Once upon a time there was a farmer who hauled his produce to market with a horse and wagon. Each year his harvest grew larger, so he kept loading more into the wagon in order to carry the bigger load. One day on his way to the market with a huge load of produce, his horse suddenly collapsed and died. And everyone wondered why the horse, which had been so reliable for so many years, should be suddenly overwhelmed by his task.

Most intimate relationships today follow the pattern shown by the farmer with his horse. We pile an ever-growing load of needs onto our intimate relationships, and then, when a relationship deteriorates under this excessive burden, we question the validity of any intimate relationship.

The institution of marriage, our traditional form of intimacy, is in deep trouble. Proposed remedies for this ailing institution include just about every reasonable and unreasonable possibility, including rigorous enforcement of the old standards of marriage; open marriage; group marriage; communal living; even the abolishment of marriage. Some people go so far as to avoid intimate relationships of any kind.

Any one of these or other remedies may work for a particular individual. These various options offer the potential for years of experimentation with different styles of relating. Some men and women move from one pattern of relating to another, wasting most of their adult lives, hoping that eventually they will find what they need. Such searching may become a life-style in itself and lead to an increasing feeling of despair. The joys, the nourishment and growth and the meaningfulness of real intimacy remain elusive.

As far back as she could remember, Jan could recall hearing her parents arguing violently at night when they thought she was asleep. She was fearful that one day her parents would carry out their often repeated threat to divorce "in spite of the children." She resolved never to have such a marriage, and even in high school her relationships with boys were dominated by her determination to avoid any relationship similar to that of her parents. She grew up with no idea of what a meaningful man-woman relationship was really like.

She pursued her search for a meaningful relationship with great determination but found those with any discord too disturbing. Others, which were indeed almost frictionless, she found boring. "The ones that turn me on I can't get along with, and the ones I can get along with bore me to death," she complained.

By the time she was nineteen she had had three relationships with men, each of which she thought would lead to real intimacy. Her sexual experience with these men was primarily motivated by her hope that this would deepen the relationship. When arguments occurred, she found herself sexually turned off, disappointed and disillusioned. She would rationalize the subsequent breakup as a good lesson and was thankful that she had found out "before it was too late."

Hank was one of those few men she found interesting and attractive but who did not initially return her interest. "I know he likes me, but he's shy," she commented to one of her friends.

It was not too difficult to approach Hank. They began to see each other exclusively, and nine months later were married. She congratulated herself that she had a good marriage, one quite different from that of her parents.

Hank had always been very intensely involved in his studies and would frequently not see Jan when he had a great deal of work to do. At first she appreciated this, but after he received his graduate degree in engineering and took a position with a large company, she began to feel resentful that he had the same intense involvement with his job that he had had with his studies. Hank shared his work activities with Jan and always explained the need to do the extra work he was frequently called upon to do. He had indeed advanced rapidly within the company.

One day Jan unexpectedly blew up at Hank, who had been out of town and called to tell her that his boss insisted he remain an extra two days to help him complete some negotiations. She was shocked by her reaction. She, who had detested arguments and fights all her life, had initiated the first real argument in her marriage. Hank loved Jan very much and sincerely tried to give her more attention. Yet his business trips and overtime were part of his job. Jan became increasingly resentful, and despite her continued resolution not to fight with Hank, she periodically blew up. She became filled with remorse when she recognized the same pattern in her marriage that she so detested in her parents'.

Although she didn't want a divorce, she felt she had no choice, since arguing was intolerable.

After her divorce she became a professional model and began dating a great many men. She was more fearful than ever and resolute against any deep involvement. Still, she longed for closeness, and when Steve, who was married, asked her out, she accepted. Not wanting any intense involvement, she felt she could overcome her loneliness by having an affair with Steve. Despite her intentions, she became deeply involved with Steve and increasingly resentful about the limited time they had together. After three years the pain was intolerable. With professional help she was able to end the relationship.

Now she decided to be more independent and to avoid exclusive relationships of any kind. She turned her interest toward her career, which by this time was quite successful. Sexually she felt free with any man she found attractive, but she continued to avoid any commitment to anyone.

One of the men she had dated on and off for three years was Frank—and she liked him. Finally, Frank convinced her that they should try living together. She was now twenty-nine and again aware of her longing for a stable relationship. She and Frank moved in together with the clear understanding that it was an experiment and each was free to date other people.

Their relationship thrived. Frank stopped dating other women. Jan would periodically date someone as a way of protecting herself. None of these men was important to her. Nevertheless, Frank became increasingly jealous and finally told Jan that he was unwilling to continue their relationship if she needed to date. Her fear of a bad marriage remained as intense as ever, and though she cared very deeply for Frank, she would not accept his demand. They separated.

After that she had several meaningful relationships but persisted in her unwillingness to risk either a broken home or having her children grow up with two unhappy parents. She continued her modeling and developed a variety of other interests. She was never without suitors, and this helped her ignore both her deep loneliness and the need to face up to her unwillingness to risk the commitment of an exclusive intimacy. She never understood what intimacy was all about and continued to be dominated by her fears and unreasonable expectations.

There is a more satisfactory way of living. I call it Creative Intimacy, a way of relating between two people in which each finds support, enhances his and her potential and at the same time protects his and her essential freedom and separate, unique identity.

Before defining Creative Intimacy further, it is necessary to define its basic ingredients: the nourishing person as opposed to the toxic person, the role of one's Intimate Other and finally the Intimacy of Two, which is the basic unit involved in Creative Intimacy.

Toxic and Nourishing Behavior: T People and N People

At any point in our life each of us does the best we can to gratify our needs and live a meaningful life. Even self-destructive attitudes and behavior represent the most effective reaction a person is able to discover *and* act on at the time in his efforts to resolve his conflicts.

Often we know in our heads or feel in our gut that what we are doing to ourselves, how we relate to others or how we allow others to relate to us leaves us feeling tense, irritable and frustrated or tired, bored and depressed. These feelings are body messages telling us that something we are doing or experiencing is toxic. Emotionally we are poisoning ourselves or allowing someone else to poison us. Toxic (T) people are those whose reactions to living are more frequently experienced in this way. The more toxic we are, the more of our experiences are frustrating, tension-producing and emotionally draining on ourselves and on those around us.

Each of us has his own pattern of toxic attitudes and behavior that can never be eliminated entirely (none of us is perfect); nor would this be necessary. However, through increasing awareness of our toxic patterns and a willingness to experiment in our search for new attitudes and behavior which may be more nourishing, we can learn how to minimize the poisonous experiences we inflict on ourselves or others or allow others to inflict on us.

T people poison themselves by self-imposed patterns of squeezing and inhibiting their spontaneity and naturalness when there are no *realistic* reasons to do so. They carry with them a variety of obsolete prohibitions and restrictions without which they would become anxious, frightened, guilt-ridden or embarrassed. They are unwilling to re-evaluate or to risk experimenting with gradually letting go of them. Although these obsolete patterns *are* self-destructive and toxic, they also protect a person from his fantasies of the catastrophic consequences that might occur if he risked giving them up. Toxic patterns typically serve as a "security blanket" at the same time that they stifle a person's aliveness and growth. T people lack the self-trust necessary to risk allowing themselves to be more open and spontaneous even though they know intellectually that therein lies the road to greater self-love and love for others. Instead they remain stuck, dominated by fantasies that there are unacceptable, even monstrous, aspects of their selves that must be kept hidden forever. They live their entire lives convinced that inside them dwells this despicable self, which would horrify everyone and lead to total alienation and isolation.

Toxic people look to others, especially their Intimate Others, to satisfy more of their needs and alleviate more of their frustrations than is realistic. Most of us, like that farmer, tend to overwork and overload our relationships and insist that they provide an unduly large proportion of our total needs for emotional nourishment. Toxic patterns develop when we look to relationships as our *primary* source of gratifying our needs and *primary* means of developing our sense of identity. T people tend to cop out on taking the responsibility for looking to themselves for these essentials and instead seek to place this burden on others. "What good is an experience if you can't share it with someone?" (That is, "I refuse to be self-reliant.") It is the T person who sees relationships as the *basic* solution to personal growth and as an antidote to his loneliness and feelings of alienation from other people and from himself as well.

Brad had no idea who he really was. Except for his feelings of emptiness and loneliness, he had little awareness of his inner self. To overcome his feelings of alienation he became a "reactor" to other people. To do anything alone was meaningless. He hardly knew whether he really enjoyed a movie or a television program until someone else told him how he, the other person, felt about it. Then Brad would pick up on the other's experience and make it his own. This was not a superficial act. Being so out of touch with himself, he simply swallowed other people's attitudes and made them his own. He avoided the full painfulness of his lack of identity and loneliness by developing a large circle of friends and engaging in as many activities as possible, all of which were initiated by others. This became his life-style for many years. He seemed busy, active and involved in the world; yet he continued to have increasing feelings of depression, which mystified him. He constantly felt he had a lump in the pit of his stomach which he could get rid of only through physical activity or tranquilizers. Being out of touch with himself, he could not see that his depression and the lump in his stomach were body messages telling him he was emotionally starving and isolated despite all the outward appearances to the contrary.

Those whose attitudes and behavior patterns are predominantly nourishing (N people) function in a manner that reflects a set of attitudes and behavior patterns opposite to those of T people. The nourishing quality of their relating elicits feelings of excitement, joy and gratification within themselves and others as well. N people are emotionally and psychologically attractive. In contrast to the depleted feeling of being emotionally drained after contact with T people, one feels enriched and energized in the presence of N people. They (N people) are more natural and spontaneous than T people. Being more self-reliant and self-nourishing, they do not dump the responsibility for meeting their needs on others. The fulfillment and gratifications an N person experiences in relating to another is a *mutually* nourishing experience. This is in marked contrast to T people, whose way of gratifying their needs in a relationship is frequently experienced by the other person as being at his expense.

In summary, the attitudes and behavior patterns of T people are characteristically phony, manipulative and deceptive. T people lack self-reliance and tend to use other people to gratify needs that legitimately are their own responsibility. Their lack of self-trust and their inner fears about what they are really like deep down diminish their naturalness and spontaneity. Consequently they are rigid and inflexible (although they usually deny this vehemently). In relating to themselves and others they are moralistic and judgmental, and they tend to think in terms of either/or (a person or idea is either good or bad), failing to see the shades of gray in between.

In contrast, N people are more open, authentic and direct in asking for what they want. They are more accepting of their selves, even of those aspects that they dislike or wish to change. They are more flexible and adaptable to change, more accepting of other people even when they disagree strongly with them. They avoid being judgmental and critical of themselves or of others. They are more trusting of themselves and humankind and more optimistic in their outlook on life.

The Intimate Other

Our Intimate Other is that special person who plays the central role in satisfying our emotional needs during some period of our adult lives. The term defines an attitude of relating with one other person which has grown in intensity and depth to the point where we know that our Intimate Other is not only special but irreplaceable—in our lives at the present time—as our prime source of security, stability and emotional nourishment.

The term Intimate Other reflects a level of relating which requires considerable time (years rather than months)

simply to allow for the necessary range of emotional inter-
actions and experiencing with the Other to occur and be as-
similated by each. Since it is toward our Intimate Other
that we have learned to feel most compatible, accepted
and trusting, these feelings reflect a lengthy process that
has developed and is continuing to develop.

We can contrast our attitude toward our Intimate Other
with what I call "instant intimacy," in which the intensity
of feelings may be as strong (e.g., in a thunder-and-lightning
romance) as in a more matured relationship but in which our
feelings have not yet had the necessary time to ripen into
a stable, broader and potentially more enduring relationship.

An Intimacy of Two

There are many kinds of intimacy, but the intimacy
between two adult peers is unique. The reasons for this
are both physiological and biological. For example, since
our eyes cannot focus on two objects at the same time (try
holding up your forefingers twelve inches apart and focusing
on both), we can give our full visual attention to only one
person at any instant. Similarly, our physiology limits the
full experiencing of contact to one other person at a time.
(Try holding hands with two people at the same time. Then
hold hands with one person. Which did you experience
more sharply?) If we understand that these facts necessarily restrict our options, we can begin to see more clearly
the problems and resolutions of an Intimacy of Two.

An Intimacy of Two is a relationship in which two adults
are committed to an interlocking dependency on each
other. The satisfactions of many of their important needs

are intertwined with each other's. In vital areas of their existence, each person is a major influence on the other. The pain, the conflicts, the frustrations of one, inevitably effect the well-being of the other in important ways. The joys, happiness and good fortune they experience are intensified by a powerful need to share these with the Other. Experientially, an essential aspect of their relationship and their individual contentment requires the well-being of the other. This is more than caring for or concern about another person whom one loves. Part of each self is so enmeshed in the other that to some extent they have a commonself—an area in which their separate identities have merged. When we experience such a relationship, each of the two knows how special the other is. That this person is *my* Intimate Other.

An enduring Intimacy of Two may not be for everyone. For adults an Intimacy of Two is an option, not a necessity. There will be times when we may be aware that other interests, activities or goals are more important and more meaningful to us. Or we may decide that we will never want this kind of relationship. All of us can only seek to discover for ourselves whether our need for an Intimacy of Two is sufficiently urgent that we choose to give up what we *must* give up if we are to sustain the commitments that an Intimacy of Two by its very nature requires.

Creative Intimacy

Briefly then, Creative Intimacy is an unending process of discovery and growth in ourselves and in the life we build with our Intimate Other. It involves a process of separate nourishment and mutual nourishment. The more we nourish ourselves, the more nourishment we have available to give to our Intimate Other. Similarly, Creative Intimacy leads to growing awareness and acceptance of our separate selves and each other *as we are*. We then no longer feel we must change either ourselves, our Intimate Other or our Intimacy of Two. In each of these we are aware of what we like *and* what we don't like.

Growth and change emerge freely and spontaneously in creative intimacy. One of the hallmarks of creative intimacy is the absence of "shoulds," "musts" or other demands upon ourselves or others.

CHAPTER

2

THE STRUCTURE OF AN INTIMACY OF TWO

An Intimacy of Two is a relationship between two people in which equality and mutual commitment constitute the essence of their relating and interacting. The legal status of their relationship (marriage), their sexual activity and other such criteria assume an aspect of superficiality compared to these two essential basics.*

Only the individual can know whether he feels the connectedness of real intimacy with another. He alone knows about his caringness, his dependence on the other for a particular kind of emotional satisfaction, and his own feelings of specialness between himself and his Intimate Other.

---

* The concept of an Intimacy of Two is valid whether the sexual orientation is heterosexual or homosexual.

In an Intimacy of Two there exists a mutual desire for an enduring stability that is based on the growth of the partners—both separately and together. The strength and stability of the relationship develops when the interaction between the two and their experiencing of each other are predominantly nourishing. And the growing feeling of emotional connectedness reflects a healthy dependency. It is a dependency that is mutually satisfying and enhances the growth of the relationship for both partners in marked contrast to toxic dependency, in which one partner avoids using and developing his own potential by placing the responsibility for his needs on the other.

The stability and permanence of an Intimacy of Two is in direct proportion to the feelings of personal growth and mutual connectedness experienced by each partner.

In an Intimacy of Two the partners do not work directly at developing a permanent relationship. They work at developing a nourishing interaction with each other—and permanence is one of the products of that supportive interaction.

Self-trust is necessary for full appreciation of the power that nourishing interaction has in building a solid foundation for a continuing relationship.

Just the awareness of the need for trust in oneself is often an effective antidote to fears that an intimate relationship might end one day for no understandable reason.

In contrast to this nourishing condition of permanence developed through open and nourishing interaction, a toxic relationship is based on poisonous games of manipulation, control and entrapment. The two partners remain "married" or connected by fears, anxieties and other feelings of insecurity and helplessness which they try to avoid by remaining together. They ignore the reality that every honest relationship is an active process, *not something concrete one can claim ownership of as if the other were a material possession.*

An Intimacy of Two has two essential characteristics. The first, as I have said, is a *commitment* toward each other based on a mutual desire for a relationship in which the life-style of each partner is significantly intertwined with that of the other. Commitment in an Intimacy of Two is part of their feeling of connectedness to each other, a mutual interdependency of equals. Each person's individuality remains foremost, and each is also aware that the well-being of his Intimate Other is essential to his own well-being. This is one characteristic that makes an Intimacy of Two unique in comparison to other love relationships.

The other essential characteristic in an Intimacy of Two is *exclusiveness.* This requires a sensitive awareness of the interconnection of the needs of each partner. And—this is very important—it includes a commitment by each partner to share certain areas of himself or herself only with the Intimate Other. These areas of exclusive relating (which will differ in every Intimacy of Two) are arrived at mutually and are based on the kind of mutual trust that permits emotional dependency.

We cannot satisfy some of our needs alone and must depend on another person.

These needs include being willing to be open and vulnerable by sharing parts of ourselves about which we are particularly anxious or sensitive. Some people do not allow themselves to feel this kind of need easily, so it is important to understand the basic need for a nourishing dependency. Each of us has areas of inner conflict—alienated parts of each of us which we deny (block off from our conscious awareness) or react to with feelings of guilt or shame. In an Intimacy of Two the *extent* of the openness and sharing of these feelings is another unique aspect that further reinforces the mutual trust that each is loved, accepted and appreciated by the other as he or she *is*.

This relationship demands exclusiveness, and that exclusiveness recognizes and accepts those aspects of relating which each partner is unwilling to allow the other to share with anyone else. For example, each may feel committed to sexual fidelity with the other and will accept the exclusive quality of this aspect of their relationship. Exclusiveness includes many things that each partner shares far more extensively with his Intimate Other than with anyone else.

An Intimacy of Two acknowledges the priorities of each with the other; their availability to each other takes precedence over their availability in other adult relationships.

Again, this is an attitude of mutual desire and willingness. Each *feels* the priority of the other.

HUSBAND (*to his wife after a weekend in which his parents had been visiting*): I like the way you responded to Mother when she wanted to take over and get you to do things her way. I know she gets under your skin sometimes, and I appreciate your patience and diplomacy when she gets domineering. But I want you to know that you are number one with me—you are the most important person in my life. I hope you and Mother can enjoy each other, but in any case, you can count on me if there ever should be any real problems between the two of you.

An Intimacy of Two is based on the desire *or* willingness of each to reach out or respond to the other as in the following example.

WIFE (*to her husband in response to his request that she give a dinner party for his boss and several important customers*): Of course I'll give the party. You know I think these parties are phony, and I don't really enjoy them. However, I know how important they are to your work.

An Intimacy of Two is characterized by the feeling of each partner that the other is clearly the one person with whom he or she has the most emotional involvement and from whom he or she both seeks and experiences the greatest amount of emotional satisfaction. Each person is aware of wanting to share much of himself with the other, and this feeling is clearly stronger than with anyone else.

Having said this, I also want to emphasize that the Intimate Other does not always have this top priority. The nourishing person has other loving, intimate relationships. Each of us chooses to share parts of ourselves and some of our interests with people other than the most important person in our life. When we have had a fight with our Intimate Other, we may seek solace from our best friend and need most to share our feelings with that person. At that moment the Intimate Other may be the last person we would feel like talking with. Similarly, we may enjoy activities that our Intimate Other doesn't want to share. One may enjoy concerts, while the other falls asleep during them. One may be a football enthusiast, while the other doesn't understand the game and is not interested in learning about it. Each may find other people with whom he clearly enjoys sharing activities more than with the Intimate Other.

Intimacy is a choice, not an inevitable way of relating. An Intimacy of Two *does* involve greater emotional risk than so-called multiple intimacies. The amount of time and energy involved in creating an Intimacy of Two unavoidably commits each person to a greater vulnerability to rejection by the other. In the same sense, their greater degree of dependence on each other for the satisfaction of so many of their needs makes them more subject to the trauma of severe emotional deprivation should the relationship end. Such an event is often experienced, particularly by the rejected partner, as leaving him or her in an emotional void. Typically this is expressed by statements such as "I feel my life is over," or "Now I have to make a whole new life for myself." In return for the emotional risk and vulnerability in an Intimacy of Two, there is a quality of relating the gratifications of which cannot be matched by any other kind of relationship.

3

THE INTIMATE SELF

A newborn infant has no hangups. He is open and honest in stating who he is and what he wants moment by moment. He has not yet learned the façades, roles and inhibitions with which he will later distort his naturalness. He says yes to his wants and no to what repels him. He says it totally and completely, with his whole body, his whole being.

Gradually he becomes aware of the frustrations his environment places on him as it increasingly restricts his freedom to be self-regulating. Becoming a social person means he must learn to squeeze himself into the patterns and expectations of the social world into which he was born. He must squeeze himself or face psychological catastrophe —this is the reality of childhood.

As the child grows stronger and more secure, he becomes less willing to endure this domination by others and increasingly asserts his own will. To the degree that he is successful in this struggle, he becomes an individual with his own identity—he discovers his Intimate Self.

A person will spontaneously function in a healthy, self-integrating fashion when he responds to the ongoing flow of his needs. The process begins in infancy with total self-centeredness—we cannot begin any other way. The totally narcissistic intimacy of infancy is the foundation for all future intimate relating.

The following list of comparative questions may help the reader determine when his way of relating to himself expresses an inner intimacy and self-love and when, in contrast, he rejects various aspects of himself, thereby creating the opposite of intimacy: the inner alienation and self-contempt of a person who rejects his self.

1. **Intimate Self:** Do I love and accept myself even though I am aware that I want to change some of my attitudes or behavior?

   or

   Rejecting Self: Do I feel unloving and rejecting toward myself when I am in touch with parts of me that I don't like?

2. **Intimate Self:** Do I feel elation and excitement when I discover things about myself of which I was previously unaware?

   or

   Rejecting Self: Do new experiences make me feel anxious and fearful that I will discover things about myself which will also be unacceptable to me?

3. **Intimate Self:** Am I interested in expanding my own awareness of myself in my quest for greater intimacy?

   or

   Rejecting Self: Even if I feel full of discontentment and frustration, would I rather leave well enough alone for fear that knowing myself more will only make things worse?

4. **Intimate Self:** Do I feel that there is no thought, feeling or impulse within me, however upsetting, that could shake my self-love and feeling that I am in control of myself?

or

Rejecting Self: Am I afraid that deep within me there are dreadful thoughts or impulses that might emerge and destroy me or isolate me from other people?

5. **Intimate Self:** Do I feel that I can take better care of myself and my needs than anyone else, however loving, possibly could?

or

Rejecting Self: Do I use my time and energy looking for someone to take over the responsibility of taking care of me and my needs?

6. **Intimate Self:** Do I allow my thoughts and feelings to emerge into full awareness?

or

Rejecting Self: Do I squeeze myself when I become aware of some unfamiliar thought or feeling emerging that might make me uncomfortable?

7. **Intimate Self:** Am I comfortable concerning what thoughts and feelings I decide to share with others as well as concerning those I will not share with anyone?

or

Rejecting Self: Do I feel guilty when I am unwilling to share parts of myself even with my most Intimate Other?

8. **Intimate Self:** Am I in touch with my inner resources and strength, and do I turn to these to resolve my anxieties, conflicts and frustrations?

or

Rejecting Self: Do I attempt to manipulate others into solving my problems and relieving my frustrations and anxieties?

9. Intimate Self: Is my quest for greater inner intimacy centered on my own growing acceptance of myself as lovable?

or

Rejecting Self: Do I keep hoping that if I can get others to love and approve of me that this in turn will lead to an increased acceptance and love within myself?

10. Intimate Self: Do I feel eager to initiate activities and thereby take responsibility for generating new experiences that may be growth-enhancing?

or

Rejecting Self: Do I frequently wait passively for external stimulation or other people to relieve my boredom and make my life more exciting?

Intimate relating begins with the self. It is a toxic fantasy to believe that we can be intimate with others when we have not learned (or are afraid) to be intimate with ourselves. Self-intimacy develops naturally when we have not been excessively poisoned by the toxic attitudes of others toward us or by toxic patterns that we inflict on ourselves.

All of us can grow toward greater love and more acceptance of ourselves, and can achieve greater self-intimacy, regardless of our age.

This is true, even when we have been filled with self-contempt or dominated by anxiety and fear as far back as we can remember.

Intimacy with one's self is basic to all intimate relating with others.

When we lack intimacy with ourselves, our identity is fragmented. We split ourselves into "acceptable" and "unacceptable" compartments. This split hampers our growth and integration into a whole person. Most typically, this is expressed by critical, disapproving attitudes. Many people spend their lives attempting to free themselves from their lack of self-acceptance and self-love by struggling to achieve recognition from others. Such endeavors rarely change their inner feelings even when they are "successful" and recognized by others. These people still do not accept themselves as they are and—no matter what respect or praise they receive from others—still do not like themselves.

Intimacy with myself grows from within. Only I can give myself this inner acceptance.

Self-love and self-intimacy are mutually enhancing. Self-love and intimacy with one's self set the stage for nourishing behavior. N people want to be nice to themselves. They enjoy taking care of themselves. N people recognize that what *they* do is central in satisfying their needs and enhancing their growth. This "self-centeredness" is exhilarating and exciting. N people, since they *are* intimate with themselves, relish being their own primary source of nourishment. Their basic strength rests on this intimate contact with and love for themselves and provides a security and stability that cannot be equaled by any relationship, however intimate, throughout their adult lives.

The inner relationship of an intimate self—the intimacy, familiarity and acceptance (regardless of whether I like each part of myself or not)—is the only relationship I know I will always have as long as I am alive.

When we are on intimate terms and enjoy a loving relationship with ourselves, then whatever the course of our relationships with others, we can always in times of adversity or rejection turn inward to our own resources and find the comfort and security that come from loving ourselves and knowing who we are. Here is an infinite reservoir of strength with which we can renew ourselves and continue to reach out to the world, making contact with others and developing new relationships.

Intimacy with one's self, then, provides an endless source of energy for establishing and sustaining intimate relationships with others. When, for whatever reasons, an intimate relationship with another ends, the intimate self knows that when he finishes mourning his loss, he can reach out again. This endless possibility for new relationships based on self-trust and self-love comes only from intimacy with one's self.

Since N people are so much more intimate with themselves, they place less of a burden on their relationships with others. This in turn creates a favorable climate for intimacy with others. Others usually sense the integrity and strength of the person who is intimate with himself and therefore feel freer to respond on the basis of their own spontaneity. The intimacy of relating on a free, unconstricted basis then flows more easily than it would otherwise. The other person knows that N people can take care of themselves and are responsible for themselves.

The person who is intimate with himself communicates through his attitudes and behavior the message that he is responsible for himself and that the other person in a relationship is not taking on an unwanted burden.

T people lack this inner intimacy. They have not discovered their own potential strength and do not believe that turning to themselves in times of deprivation, rejection or despair will bring comfort and strength. Instead, in their intimate relationships, they seek security and stability. The more desperation they feel, the greater the likelihood that the other partner will feel burdened or pressured—possibly beyond his supportive strength.

Warning: Beware of the person who sends the message, implicit or explicit, "I want someone to take care of me." Chances are he or she lacks inner intimacy and feelings of stability and self-love.

Many people are strangers to themselves because they live out their lives paralyzed by the fear of what they would discover if they sought greater awareness of themselves. Yet inner intimacy is the gateway to a richer and more meaningful life. An "intimate self" is a person who has moved down this road to some extent and who, even more importantly, wants to continue the process of self-discovery throughout his entire life. He sees this process of expanding awareness as one that offers endless possibilities for adding greater meaning to his life.

As a person grows toward greater intimacy with himself, experiencing becomes increasingly richer. He discovers more dimensions and greater depth in all his experiences. He is not driven to search for new stimulation in his external world, because the richness of his life is based *primarily* on his inner experiencing. In contrast, those who lack intimacy with themselves (T people) must continually work harder at seeking new experiences in order to keep their lives meaningful and interesting, since the depth of their experiences is much more shallow. They seek quantity of experiences (and relationships) at the cost of quality and depth.

Each of us continually chooses between seeking and avoiding greater intimacy (contact and awareness) with ourselves. When we are anxious, fearful or depressed, avoidance is frequently the most expedient resolution. We discover our own methods (alcohol, drugs, work) for relieving our immediate pain. However, this comfort is bought at the price of limiting the meaning, vitality and excitement that we are capable of experiencing. In addition, the pressure of these walled-off parts of ourselves continue to push for expression. We cannot really escape from ourselves and the pain of our fears and anxieties.

To Grow or Not to Grow

Maturing is the process of ripening toward one's fullest potentials. N people feel joyous, excited and optimistic about their limitless potential for new discoveries in their quest for a growing inner intimacy. At the same time they reject the attitude that they "should" grow or "should" fulfill as many of their potentials as possible. The belief that it is our *duty* to achieve as much growth as possible is a toxic attitude. Growing itself can be either nourishing or toxic. When we bite off more growth than we can assimilate, we poison ourselves. Overstimulation and an excess of experiencing tend to become toxic. In this sense, growth becomes toxic when it is motivated by external demands that short-circuit the self-regulating processes that otherwise function spontaneously within us.

We do not always *need* to grow or *need* greater inner intimacy. Rather, when we are intimate with ourselves, we are aware that these are options that are available to us, not necessities.

The N person does not make a decision to grow or not to grow. His awareness of his experiencing self and his contact with himself and the world around him *are* the growth process that leads toward greater intimacy within.

Becoming intimate with one's self means discovering what "fits." Nourishing ourselves means assimilating what feels natural so that it becomes part of us, and rejecting what doesn't fit in order to avoid poisoning ourselves with alien attitudes and behavior patterns.

Although Frank had been the star pitcher in high school, in college he reluctantly agreed to try football after much persuasion by his coach. During a game, he dislocated his shoulder. He recovered fully, but he felt apprehensive about hurting his shoulder again and no longer enjoyed the game. He began to play poorly. His coach reassured him that it might take a little time, but he would eventually be his old self again. By the end of the season, Frank's fear of injury still plagued him. The following year, he went out for baseball instead.

The intimate self discovers his way *as* he moves through life.

Frank's decision was no earth-shaking event in his life. Rather, it was typical of the kind of everyday situation in which we can choose to respect our own integrity by accepting what we want and rejecting what we don't want. This *is* intimate relating to one's self. Frank might have chosen to poison himself by giving in to his anxiety about what his coach, teammates or friends might think about his dropping football. Indeed, some of his friends did feel that he had "chickened out." Giving in to such fears is a way of denying one's self.

Life is movement and change from birth to death. For some it is mostly struggle, anxiety and frustration. Others function with more grace and flow more easily with the currents of their inner selves and the world in which they live.

T people live their lives as if they were in a race. They dissipate themselves in endless conflict and make their lives an uphill struggle. When they are not actively engaged in "combat," they are anticipating and preparing for future strife and catastrophe.

We are being toxic to ourselves when we expect life to be like a roller coaster where we just sit passively and enjoy the journey to its end. Equally unrealistic is the notion that life is a struggle in which we climb one treacherous mountain after another, hoping one day to discover a peaceful valley. That, too, is a kind of craziness—the craziness of those who lack intimacy within themselves and live under the domination of the fear of unknown external forces and imaginary enemies.

The Yes-No Process

Awareness of our needs is the spark plug that activates all our behavior. Through awareness of the consequences of our actions, we discover what is nourishing for us and what is toxic. We discover what kinds of attitudes and behavior patterns suit us best. And we make our choices accordingly. In this way, all of us can evolve our own style of intimate relating to ourselves:

With sufficient awareness, I discover that I am the most central, active force determining my personal existence. Only when I have made this discovery can I commit myself to the responsibility of maintaining intimate contact with myself.

The more acute and constant our awareness, the more effectively we can say yes to our needs—a nourishing act—*and* avoid poisoning ourselves by saying no to what we find to be toxic.

Intimacy within ourselves is necessary for the growth of our identity. Developing a sense of identity, taking shape as a unique person, is the result of our pattern of yes-and-no responses to ourselves and our environment. We can experience real contact and a sense of definiteness (I know who I am!) only by knowing what we want, which also means knowing what we don't want. Our effectiveness is in saying yes and no to what we want and what we don't want. All behavior choices, however complex, involve this process of reaching out for nourishment and rejecting or eliminating what is toxic.

The effective functioning of the yes-no process is the essence of healthy responsiveness. It is a hallmark of the intimate self.

The person who is intimate with himself has a healthy "yes" attitude toward his needs. He sees life as a flow of experiences and change. He feels harmony between his ongoing flow of needs and his responsiveness to himself. Saying yes to his needs is then initiated with a minimum of conflict and anxiety.

Over a period of time, most of us experience widely contrasting, even conflicting attitudes and behavior patterns (consistency is not a human quality). The Intimate Self makes these transitions between varying needs and moods more easily than the person who is out of touch with his feelings. The Intimate Self flows in his responsiveness from one feeling to another: from excitement to quietude, from joy to sorrow, from anger to love. He just does it. He does not need to explain or justify himself. He simply lives his life, *and* in this way his living is greatly simplified and more alive and exciting.

Saying no is an *active* process of avoiding, rejecting or expelling what is experienced as toxic or ungratifying. The "no" signals tell the person when he is being poisonous or allowing himself to be poisoned.

Saying no is absolutely essential if we are to be on intimate terms with ourselves.

The Intimate Self uses his power to protect his well-being and maintain his integrity as a person. Although none of us can ever fully satisfy all his needs, "no" responses also help us avoid the distractions of lesser needs which would otherwise hamper our ability to satisfy our more important needs. It is the "no" process that enables us to avoid fragmenting ourselves by patterns of overinclusiveness (greediness). In our relating to others, a lack of selectivity (refusing to say no) results in an excessive number of superficial relationships, with the result that the potential richness of any of them is never realized. A person may have dozens of "friends" yet lack intimate involvement with any one.

When I won't say yes, I lose the self-initiating behavior I need in order to provide myself with emotional nourishment. When I won't say no, I fail to protect myself against toxic intrusions by others.

During childhood, development of intimacy with the self is enhanced or hampered by our experiences with others, particularly the most significant adults in our lives, usually our mother and father. The process of becoming an Intimate Self, of relating to one's self with love and care, is often disrupted by a toxic attitude of parents.

The prevalent attitude of parents is that selfishness is a dirty word.

Children are often taught to ignore or reject their intuitive "no" messages. Parents foster the suppression of the "no" process in their children principally through techniques that induce guilt and shame. They often manipulate their children to fulfill their (the parents') own needs and in this way suppress the development of healthy "no" functioning in their children.

BILLY: Will you please tell Jimmy (*Billy's younger brother*) to stay out of my room and not to touch my things when I'm not there? (*A healthy "no" response to protect his private space from intrusions.*)

PARENT: Why must you children be so selfish; why can't you learn to share your things with each other?

BILLY: Jimmy messes up my stuff. He takes things out of my room and loses them. It's my room, and they're my things. Why can't I be the one to decide who gets to use them?

PARENT: Well, you're not here a lot of the time, and Jimmy gets bored. I'm busy, and I don't have time for him, so why can't you let him go into your room and enjoy himself?

BILLY: Why can't Jimmy go out and make friends like I do? Why can't he play with his own stuff?

PARENT: I'm sick and tired of your selfishness. Why can't you be considerate of me for a change? (*I'm going to use my superior power to say "yes" to what I want and thereby frustrate your need to say "no" to what you don't want.*)

Often parents instill guilt feelings in their children for rejecting others. (Billy is "bad" because he does not let Jimmy play with his things. He would be "good" if he acquiesced.) Parents also teach their children to avoid saying no to others, or to avoid accepting being told no by another, as if the need to reject someone, or the necessity to accept rejection, were wrong. This hampers the child's ability to learn to cope with an obvious reality of life.

When a child bumps his head the parent can do nothing but comfort him until the pain subsides. Yet when he cries, parents often refuse to accept his need to cry until he is finished. They will say, "Stop. Stop crying. It doesn't help." Often this occurs because the crying makes *them* uncomfortable. The child spontaneously says yes to his pain and expresses it by crying, while the parents seek to force a "no" response on him. Gradually the child learns to suppress what he is told is unacceptable.

LAURA (*talking to herself using the empty-chair technique**): "You're far from perfect, Laura. You have a lot of things you could do for yourself, but I love you anyway. Laura, I have a lot of expectations for you; I'd like you to be better in a lot of ways, and I think you can, and I still like you even though you're not perfect. I *love* you even though you're not perfect. Well, Laura, even

---

* A role-playing method frequently used in Gestalt therapy to enhance awareness and contact with oneself.

though there's a lot of times that I don't *like* you, I
always *love* you.

THERAPIST: You sound embarrassed to admit you love yourself. As if you don't deserve to.

LAURA: I do believe I was taught to feel I was unlovable and
that I eventually began to act as if I did not deserve love.
I was one of those kids at a party who wouldn't come out
and get the ice cream and cake. I'd wait 'til last, or they'd
have to kind of coax me. When I was real little, I remember, I used to get up on a chair and sing "Happy Birth-
day" to myself. It was after that that I started getting
messages not to do that. I remember when I was a kid
that no matter what I did that was right, it was what was
wrong that was noticed. I really see that. Christmas Day I
had a lot of people over. There were trillions of dishes
left, and I did almost all of them—except for eight wine
glasses, when I kind of pooped out. I found myself making an excuse about the eight damn wine glasses! I
remember that if I got all A's in school and one B, I got
asked how come I got one B.

Those who have never learned how to avoid, eliminate,
or otherwise protect themselves against toxic intrusions from
others lack inner intimacy.

**When we lack intimacy with ourselves we spend our
time in activities we don't enjoy, being with people
we don't like and relating in ways that we experience
as toxic.**

By the time David was of school age, he had learned to ignore himself almost totally. "Whatever I did was always wrong. I never seemed to do anything right." David was referring to the rigorous, demanding discipline imposed by his parents. David grew up under the constant threat of punishment. ("God knows our thoughts, and don't you ever forget it. You had best start repenting while there's still time.")

David could not remember when he wasn't terrified at doing a wrong thing. He was only seven when he decided that his only chance for survival was to be a perfectly good boy. His method was to do nothing unless he was told to. He would come home from school, sit down in the kitchen and wait for his mother to tell him what to do. When she was preoccupied with other things, he would sit for hours scarcely moving. Sometimes she would ask him if he wanted a glass of milk or something to eat. He would timidly reply, "Yes, if it's all right, ma'am." When she was irritated, she would tell him to get out of her sight, and he would go in the yard and sit by himself. He was fearful of venturing away from home lest this incur the anger of his parents.

Although he had no friends, David did well in school and was praised by his teachers. No one seemed to notice the blank, apathetic look on his face. He rarely smiled, even when given a treat—except when one of his parents, usually in the presence of company, would say, "Smile, David, what's the matter with you?"

In high school he was simply considered shy and continued to play the role of an obedient child. He entered the service, where he was nicknamed "Dumb David" because of his willingness to do dirty jobs any time his sergeant called for volunteers.

For all practical purposes David appeared to have no mind of his own, no identity, no ability to respond to his own needs or say no to others. He was constantly provoked by the other men as if it were a challenge to get a reaction out of him. Such attempts had always been futile until one day one of the men jabbed him in the buttocks with his bayonet, David flew into an explosive rage and severely beat his assailant, whom he might have killed if others had not pulled him off. David himself was taken to the psychiatric ward. There he was filled with anguish and remorse and spent hours begging the Lord to forgive him.

His treatment was combined with a close working relationship with a minister, who helped David adopt a more loving, less fearful attitude toward God. For the first time in his life, he began to feel he was a person with the right to respond to his own needs. Finally he was learning to love his self. After his discharge he went to divinity school and became an ordained minister. He continued in psychotherapy throughout these years and eventually established a counseling and guidance clinic for one of the large churches in a major city.

Ideally, within the limits of reality, a person would do what he wants. He would flow with his self. He would postpone some gratifications because of other needs or goals more important to him. His feelings of responsibility would also be part of his identity, part of the natural flow of his self. His conduct and attitudes toward himself and others would then be self-regulating.

The Intimate Self functions in a manner that is least disrupting to a person's self. If he feels depressed, he allows himself to experience his depression. While he does not wallow in it, neither does he fight *against* it. He flows *with* it. He considers his depression part of his experiential world at that moment, communicating a message of deprivation just as any other need makes itself known by some body message. The more a person is willing to respond to his needs in this way, i.e., the more intimate he is with himself, the greater his likelihood of obtaining satisfaction and moving on to other needs, activities and interests.

Earl, thirty-five, had always been lonely, and he was fearful that he always would be. A sensitive man, he was aware of those people he felt attracted toward and really wanted to know. Yet he would form friendships with people who were never really his first choice. He paralyzed himself with his fear of rejection and would not reach out either to other men with whom he felt a real kinship or to the women he found particularly attractive. Invariably he was chosen instead of initiating the choosing.

During grade school he had fantasies of being accepted by boys he admired, but he never approached them. He selected his friends from those who approached him. During his childhood his family had moved three times. Each move was a dreadful experience for him because of his loneliness and his fear of reaching out to make new friends.

When he began dating in high school, the same pattern prevailed. In this way he avoided his fear of loneliness while continuing to frustrate himself by not seeking the kind of relationship he knew he needed and wanted.

This pattern continued in college. He would date one girl at a time until his dissatisfaction would suddenly erupt and he would end the relationship. At some point when their relationship seemed to be going well he would blow up at some minor incident and never see the girl again. What had happened, and he knew it, was that he reached the point where he could no longer continue the relationship. He did not have the courage to tell the girl honestly that their relationship was over.

In graduate school he began going with Louise, who

seemed more acceptable than most of the women he had dated. He felt secure with her since he knew she cared for him a great deal more than he cared for her. Two years later they were married. For the first time in his life Earl felt a real sense of belonging and security. To his surprise he even felt love for Louise and decided that he had made a good choice and had found the enduring intimacy he had always wanted. Actually, he was more in love with the security of their relationship.

Feeling more secure now, Earl began taking more risks in reaching out to people, and he began to find that they did respond to him. Eventually this kindled his old awareness that his relationship with Louise was lacking in the emotional depth he now began to experience with people with whom *he* initiated a relationship.

Shortly after he received his law degree, he met Vickie, a secretary in the law firm that had hired him. Vickie was married and flirtatious. She and Earl began to have an affair. Earl felt quite attracted to Vickie, but at the same time he knew that here again was not really the woman he wanted. Both Vickie and Earl had deteriorating marriages, and their relationship with each other accelerated the deterioration. Vickie left her husband and moved into her own apartment, while Earl began fighting with Louise and staying out at night in open defiance. Again he was not willing to be honest and end the marriage. He hoped that Louise would become sufficiently outraged at his behavior to do this for him. Louise, however, felt that whatever Earl was going through would run its course. One day, in his characteristic style, Earl blew up at Louise over some trivial matter and moved out.

He proposed to Vickie and was shocked by her refusal. She loved him but, because of her own anxiety, was not ready to make such a commitment.

They saw each other now and then for a period of four

years. Earl also dated other women. Finally he felt strong enough to break completely with Vickie.

He felt more able to tolerate his loneliness and was now more resolute about not getting involved with someone with whom he did not sincerely feel he might find the kind of relationship he had always known he wanted. He now began to genuinely enjoy women for the first time in his life. He was learning how to avoid frustrating himself and to nourish his own emotional needs more fully. He was also more open, honest and giving with women.

Nevertheless, as he put it years later, "I needed to poison myself one more time before I really woke up!" When he met Ann he was immediately aware of her loneliness and near desperation. She had just broken a two-year engagement, and his empathy for her caused him to lose touch with his own needs. Almost from the beginning Ann wanted an exclusive relationship. In response to her neediness Earl again lost touch with himself. The next two years were another roller coaster relationship. Earl, faithful to his old pattern, finally blew up and abruptly stopped seeing Ann.

Finally, Earl was ready to confront himself with his fear of loneliness. He was no longer willing to continue his game playing relationships. He dated no one for about five months and learned to tolerate his feelings of loneliness rather than continue to escape into meaningless relationships. When he did begin dating again he would approach those women he found most interesting and attractive. When he wasn't really interested he would stop dating that woman. Now he was nourishing himself more than he ever had—and poisoning himself less—in spite of his continuing anxiety about his loneliness. He was willing to risk rejection rather than detour himself from seeking the kind of relationship he knew he wanted.

He could feel his voice quiver and his hands trembling when he called Donna, whom he had met at a cocktail party. He felt she was the most attractive woman he had ever met. As luck would have it, she was interested in someone else.

Rather than crumbling under this rejection Earl told her he would call again in a month or two since she implied that things were not going well between her and her boyfriend. Some time later he heard that Donna had broken her engagement. Immediately he called her, and they began seeing each other. Their relationship eventually led to marriage.

Conversely, the more we fight a need and the more we interrupt ourselves, the stronger the need grows. In so doing, we are saying no to our self and increasing our state of tension. We become increasingly self-poisoning (the opposite of intimacy) as more and more of our strength is invested in this kind of impasse. The accumulating pressure will inevitably force its way out as the impasse continues. It will be increasingly expressed in distressing symptoms, body messages reflecting the deprivation that results when we refuse to flow with our self.

In the case of Earl above, the body message that gave him clear signals that he was poisoning himself occurred primarily in the pit of his stomach. He would feel his anxiety as a knot (tying him up) when he wanted to approach an attractive woman and was too frightened. At times when he was in a relationship that he knew was only an escape from his loneliness, he would experience a feeling of nausea. In therapy he discovered that his body was telling him to vomit up these relationships.

Another body message that he was frequently aware of but tried to ignore was the fidgeting of his feet. He would find his toes wiggling and, literally, knew that he wanted to run from a relationship he didn't want. The way he frustrated himself and turned his anger in on himself led to severe depressions. Particularly in his relationship with Vickie he, at times, felt a physical weakness that was so severe that he consulted his physician on several occasions. In therapy he learned the meaning of this body message; he was exhausting himself in a relationship that did not give him the nourishment he needed.

Psychic Detours

Lack of intimate contact with ourselves leads to "psychic detours." Our behavior is then out of harmony with our most important needs. We use our time, energy and resources in ways that lack the meaningfulness we can experience only when our behavior is integrated with the mainstream of our evolving needs.

Some detours are inevitable in discovering what is most meaningful to us. No one has such intimate contact with his inner self that he always knows what he needs or how to respond. It is a toxic attitude to expect that whatever we do "should" turn out well. Detours (mistakes) are inevitable and offer valuable discoveries from which a person can learn what doesn't fit *his* ways of being.

Major detours are important disruptions in our quest for a life-style that is responsive to and enhancing of greater intimacy with ourselves. Often these detours are difficult to alter since they involve commitments from which the person cannot easily extricate himself.

A crisis developed when Raymond decided he wanted to study medicine even though his father insisted that he join the family business: "I built this business for you, son; after all, what do I need it for? You're the one who has his future ahead of him. Why make your life difficult when you have a ready-made opportunity to step into?"

This argument flared repeatedly and ended in an angry standoff each time. Raymond was accepted into medical school but needed financial help until he could find a job. His father indignantly refused. As the deadline for enrollment came closer, the arguments became more violent. One day, in a fit of extreme rebelliousness and anger, Raymond enlisted in the Marines. His father was devastated and finally admitted defeat.

In his rage Raymond was intent on demonstrating to his father once and for all that he could not be forced to do anything he didn't want to do. While he demonstrated this in a convincing manner, he also created a major disruption of his own plans. Although his need to rebel against his father was understandable, it was still his responsibility that he had detoured himself away from what he really wanted.

A threat to my intimate relationship with myself is often experienced as a clear feeling that "I won't tolerate this. It would be devastating to me."

Chronic Detours

Some people waste years of their lives—or their entire lives—in a life-style that violates their own integrity. When this happens they usually feel, however vaguely, that something basic is always missing. In some important area they lack, or have lost, intimate contact with themselves and at least some of their essential needs.

The chronically detoured person victimizes himself by continuing a pattern of behavior that has become a major disruption in his quest for a nourishing life-style. As long as he is unaware (or unwilling to recognize) that he is violating a major aspect of his self, the chronic detour will continue. Even when he is aware of what he is doing, he may still rationalize or justify continuing his toxic existence. Frequently a person realizes that he is wasting his life in activities or relationships that are poisonous and disruptive to him. Yet he continues to poison himself and wallow in his frustration.

T people remain stuck in chronic detours. Their vacillating, ineffective behavior reflects the self-poisoning attitude of avoiding intimate contact with themselves and their own basic needs. They may complain of their unhappiness and make well-meant promises, but they fail to act.

Rick had always loved working on engines and repairing cars. When he graduated from high school he was offered a job as a mechanic in a nearby garage. But Sue, who had been going with Rick for over two years, told him frankly that she didn't want to marry a "grease monkey." Rick became a salesman for a large company, and he and Sue were married. A few years later, with Sue's encouragement, he accepted a job with another firm at a much higher salary and became a successful sales executive. He also developed a chronic ulcer, which at times required hospitalization. He had always been aware of the stress and strain of his job. His favorite form of relaxation (and his real interest) still remained working on cars.

When Rick's ulcer became increasingly severe, he began to see a therapist. He had long been aware that his stomach reacted badly to the stress of sales meetings, road trips and the numerous social functions he attended in order to maintain good relationships with his customers. In therapy he became more acutely aware of the contrasting feeling of relaxation and pleasure when he was home and, particularly, when he worked in his garage: "When I have a week off during the slow season and do nothing but stay home and work on cars, I feel just great and my stomach does too." He became increasingly aware of his joyless, frustrating life and eventually confronted himself with the poisonous effects of his job. However, Sue reminded him that he had more financial obligations than ever, including putting their three children through college. He reassured himself that "Once my kids are out of college, I'm going to quit and open a small auto repair shop. Until then, I really can't afford a lower income. I've put up with my job this long, I guess I can stand it a little longer."

Usually those people (like Rick) who live a chronically toxic life-style are unwilling to rebel sufficiently to break free. Instead they remain vulnerable to the demands and manipulations of others, which drain their strength further and leave them increasingly vulnerable to other psychic detours.

The person on a chronic detour lives a life-style in which he sacrifices intimacy with his self. By responding to lesser needs or the manipulations of others, he fails to live harmoniously with his intimate self.

When I lose touch with my Intimate Self (who I am and what I want), I may give up the quest for experiencing life more fully and stay stuck in the narrow world of a limited existence largely dictated by obsolete habits or the manipulations of others.

It is not possible for me to relate to others intimately and allow (and enjoy) their full expression of themselves if I have not yet discovered how to do this for myself. An Intimacy of Two begins with an intimacy of one.

4

ONE-TO-ONE INTIMACY

An Intimacy of Two is not like any other kind of relationship. It offers the potential for an incomparable depth of sharing and continuity of relating. It is the ultimate extension of that most intimate of all experiences, intimacy with one's self. Just as the Intimate Self cannot possibly share all the inner richness of his fantasies and his experiencing of the world around him, the potential richness of sharing when two adults are truly intimate is unimaginable. It is unmatched by any other kind of relationship.

Our Intimate Other is that special person with whom we share ourselves most, upon whom we are most emotionally dependent and to whom we are, in turn, most available. He or she is the person with whom we are the most open, vulnerable and trusting, the person with whom we most want to commit ourselves to a mutually shared life-style.

Just as the intimate self is aware of those aspects of his self which he shares with no one, so too he is aware of the specialness of his sharing of himself with his Intimate Other.

Only we know within ourselves when we are involved in an intimate relationship with another person. What looks like intimacy to others is frequently an empty or dead relationship to one or both of the people involved. In an Intimacy of Two there is a distinct, mutually experienced pattern of attitudes and behavior. When we are aware of a growing intimacy toward someone and we also pay attention to how *he or she* relates to us, we can increase our awareness of whether the other person is also relating to us initimately or whether we are involved in a one-way-street relationship.

How Do I Know I'm in an Intimate Relationship?

1. **Intimate Relating:** Do I feel a sense of harmony and acceptance when I am with my Intimate Other?
   or
   Am I mainly hoping to feel this way while actually experiencing a good deal of tension, conflict and frustration?

2. **Intimate Relating:** Do I see myself as a whole person seeking a relationship that will broaden and enrich my life and add new dimensions to it?

or

Do I feel an incompleteness concerning my own identity and look to "my other half" to fill this lack within myself?

3. **Intimate Relating:** Am I aware of a depth of feeling and caring which I experience in numerous ways in our interaction with each other?

or

Is our relating largely perfunctory and void of expressions of real feelings toward each other?

4. **Intimate Relating:** Is our relationship expanding into new areas of shared interest and interaction?

or

Is our relating increasingly routine, unvarying or even monotonous?

or

5. **Intimate Relating:** Is our sexual relating an expression of our mutual love and a growing connectedness between us?

or

Is sex largely a physical gratification?

6. **Intimate Relating:** Do I experience our lovemaking as part of our spontaneous way of relating to each other?

or

Is our lovemaking dominated by techniques, preoccupation with performance or a search for new sexual "turn-ons"?

7. **Intimate Relating:** Do I feel a sense of security and trust toward my Intimate Other?

or

Am I aware of vague feelings of distrust, suspiciousness and a need to guard myself against the other person?

8. **Intimate Relating:** Is there a mutual spontaneous desire for exclusiveness in our relating to each other?

or

Do either of us resent exclusive relating with the limits it imposes upon our relationships and ways of relating with others?

9. **Intimate Relating:** Am I aware of *wanting* to give my time and energy to our relationship?

or

Do I feel I am sacrificing myself when I lack as much time as I would like for other relationships and activities?

10. **Intimate Relating:** Do I realize that at times I myself or my Intimate Other will feel hostile, unloving or detached without feeling that our entire relationship is in jeopardy?

or

Am I under the illusion that an Intimacy of Two means constant closeness and contact with each other regardless of our separate moods and other needs?

11. **Intimate Relating:** Are my giving *and* my responsiveness to being given to by my Intimate Other, one of the most joyful aspects of our relationship?

or

Do I find that giving is burdensome and that it takes effort for me to give *or* receive?

12. **Intimate Relating:** Are our most important needs, the kind of relationship and the life-style we each want most, included within the area of our mutual goals?

or

Are there vital areas of our separate selves and our needs which are antagonistic so that one or both of us is apt to experience major deprivations regardless of which life-style we choose?

13. **Intimate Relating:** Am I interested in some of the separate experiences my Intimate Other relates to me, and do I feel this same need to share some of my separate experiences with him or her?

or

Am I essentially uninterested in the experiences of my Intimate Other and only act the role of a good listener?

14. **Intimate Relating:** Is there an ongoing dialogue between us which expresses the continuing enhancement of our intimacy?

or

Are we under the illusion that an Intimacy of Two, once it has survived for some length of time, can finally be taken for granted?

15. **Intimate Relating:** In my day-to-day contact with my Intimate Other, do I experience warm and loving moments that spontaneously arise under various circumstances?

or

Is our intimate contacting more or less scheduled for certain times and occasions?

16. **Intimate Relating:** Do I *and* my Intimate Other share areas of our separate selves which are embarrassing or in some way threatening to reveal?

or

Do we share only those parts of our separate selves about which we are comfortable and avoid revealing anything that we fear will put us in a bad light?

17. **Intimate Relating:** Do I enjoy feeling that my Intimate Other and I are increasingly special to each other in many ways?

or

In spite of our intimacy does either of us feel threatened by feelings of growing mutual dependency?

18. **Intimate Relating:** Is part of my special feeling toward my Intimate Other a particularly strong urge to give to him or her?

    or

    Is my feeling of caring and giving similar to that which I have for other people for whom I also care?

19. **Intimate Relating:** Am I aware and concerned about the well-being and satisfaction of the needs of my Intimate Other?

    or

    Do I take a "that's your problem" attitude and feel only moderately concerned about his or her well-being?

20. **Intimate Relating:** Do I feel a growing sense of mutual commitment and exclusiveness in various areas of our relating?

    or

    Am I satisfied with few limits on our separate relating to other people and unconcerned about the future direction of our relationship?

21. **Intimate Relating:** Am I unwilling to manipulate or exploit my Intimate Other into satisfying my needs regardless of my ability to do so?

    or

    Am I basically concerned with getting what I want out of the relationship with little regard for how this affects the other person?

22. **Intimate Relating:** Is the other person the one I trust most and feel more open with than with anyone else in the world?

or

Am I equally open and trusting toward close friends or relatives?

23. **Intimate Relating:** Is the other person clearly the one with whom I most want to share more of myself than with anyone else?

or

Is there no special gratification in sharing my intimate feelings and experiences with him or her as compared to the gratification I feel with other people with whom I also have a close relationship?

24. **Intimate Relating:** Am I aware of wanting a mutual commitment and an enduring relationship with my Intimate Other?

or

Do I feel that such commitments are toxic and stifling to my personal growth and sense of identity?

25. **Intimate Relating:** While experiencing the now, do we share plans and hopes for the future?

or

Are we exclusively relating in the present and either avoid or are not interested in sharing thoughts and feelings about our future relationship?

26. **Intimate Relating:** Do we openly share our views on what each of us considers to be important values, goals and acceptable patterns of behavior in a relationship?

or

Does either or both of us feel that we each have a right to do our own thing and avoid confronting ourselves or each other with possible conflicts in this area?

27. **Intimate Relating:** Am I aware that our shared activities are far more meaningful because of our mutual participation?

or

Are only the activities themselves meaningful and our sharing minimal?

28. **Intimate Relating:** Is my feeling of love and connectedness to my Intimate Other the principal motivation in my wanting a one-to-one relationship?

or

Do I want the relationship with my Intimate Other *because* he or she does so much for me and satisfies so many of my needs?

29. **Intimate Relating:** Is my giving an expression of my love and caring which emerges spontaneously from within me as one of my needs?

or

Is my giving motivated by my fear and anxiety that I *must* keep my Intimate Other happy or our relationship will end?

30. **Intimate Relating:** Do I feel that whatever gratifications I give up because of my commitment to my Intimate Other are more than compensated for by the fulfillment I experience?

or

Do I feel I sacrifice various gratifications because I fear the repercussions if I don't?

31. **Intimate Relating:** If I were rejected by an Intimate Other would I feel a deep sense of loss and mourning?

or

Would I only experience brief pain or sadness and then proceed into a new intimate relationship?

32. **Intimate Relating:** Is our relationship based on continuing mutual feelings of spontaneously wanting to remain in our Intimacy of Two?

or

Is our relationship sustained largely because of past promises to each other or because of present obligations and practicalities?

An Intimacy of Two implies a mutual recognition of the existence of important areas of exclusiveness as well as a definite priority each enjoys with the other. These qualities of mutual commitment are intrinsic in one-to-one intimacy.

Next to intimacy with one's self, an Intimacy of Two is the most essential relationship in seeking a nourishing life.

One hallmark of an Intimacy of Two is the *mutual* satisfaction they experience in their sharing together of similar emotional-need patterns and life-styles.

Part of the uniqueness of an Intimacy of Two is the free-choice basis on which two people come together and stay together. An Intimacy of Two sustains itself and thrives on the mutual nourishment the two people generate between themselves.

Any coercive force or pressure, whatever its source, is contrary to the essential spontaneity necessary for an Intimacy of Two.

Jeff was deeply in love with Martha when they married. He was also very ambitious and fully aware of the opportunities Martha's wealthy father provided. These fortunate circumstances became destructive to their relationship when Jeff became increasingly hesitant in expressing his resentments to Martha for fear of jeopardizing their marriage and with it his career and future in her father's company. The matter had never come up and was strictly a fear Jeff created through his own fantasies. Nevertheless he felt a "pressure to avoid arguments" with Martha. His suppressed resentments became increasingly destructive to their Intimacy.

An Intimacy of Two brings new dimensions of meaningfulness into the lives of each. A new quality of experience emerges through their mutual sharing which cannot be experienced separately by either. This emerging quality is an endless source of nourishment and growth both for the relationship and for each person as a separate individual.

It is this mutual satisfaction of needs which an Intimacy of Two can provide which enables each individual to accept a commitment to the other without a sense of sacrifice or deprivation.

Intimacy is an attitude, a way of being and relating to another with special closeness, trust and connectedness. Many people get stuck in their quest for intimacy because of the false idea that the principal yardstick of intimacy is the amount of time two people spend together and the duration of the relationship. ("Of course we're intimate; we've been married, living in the same house and sleeping in the same bed for twenty years.")

There are millions of couples who continue living together for years even though the intimate quality of their relationship long since died.

Others believe that a declaration of intent ("I love you") carries with it the implication that an intimate relationship now exists. Or that the key to intimate relating is to present oneself as an attractive package.

Brenda was only thirty-five when she divorced Jack, she had no intention of remaining single the rest of her life. She was still quite attractive and youthful-looking. Even the plastic surgeon tried to talk her out of—or at least into postponing—the face lift she insisted on having. Her new wardrobe, which she really could not afford, she steadfastly maintained was "an investment in finding husband number two." Lastly, as part of her campaign to remarry, she relentlessly questioned her girlfriends about the likes and dislikes of men with whom they arranged blind dates for her.

Toxic people often use a great deal of time and energy trying to learn techniques in order to discover the "secret" of successful relating. One can use up a lifetime pursuing one such gimmick after another, sincerely believing that "There must be an easy way if only I can find it."

Those who seek meaningful relationships through various gimmicks and "how-to-do-it" techniques live under the illusion that first capturing the interest of another and then becoming emotionally involved with that person are the major obstacles to meaningful intimate relating.

Sustaining an Intimacy of Two demands a continuing interest in building the relationship. This is a process of discovering new ways of relating as well as a deepening and broadening of the older nourishing ways of interacting. It also includes letting go of patterns of interacting that were nourishing in the past but are now obsolete and toxic.

Wanda was working as an executive secretary when she met Phil, an engineer some ten years older than she. They began dating almost immediately. Before she met Phil, Wanda had inherited a small house in a rustic area within commuting distance of her work. She loved the feeling of remoteness and quiet. Phil, too, enjoyed it and moved in with her about six months after they met. Wanda was rather introverted and had an air of tranquility and joyfulness Phil found very attractive. Phil was ambitious and often felt frustrated because the engineering positions open to him were limited. He had wanted to continue in graduate school but could not afford it. His discontentment with himself began to affect their relationship. Despite Wanda's reassurances, Phil continued to feel anxious about the limited level of his income and the anticipation that the things he would like to do in his life would not be possible without further education.

Wanda and Phil established a truly intimate relationship, which both valued and appreciated. Wanda was increasingly concerned about Phil's frustration and offered to support him if he wanted to return to graduate school. Phil was initially reluctant. It was difficult for Wanda to assure him that she wanted to do this for him. Phil began a Ph.D. program while still managing to work part time. This, combined with a small scholarship and student loans, enabled them to manage. Four years later Phil had his Ph.D. Both were delighted and continually aware that these were good years, joyfully spent together.

Phil returned to the same company with a much higher salary and a promising future. At some point a few months after Phil received his doctorate, he and Wanda decided to marry. They spent the next few years traveling during their vacations, enlarging the house and planting a small orchard.

When Wanda gave birth to twin girls, both she and Phil were delighted. A new phase of their life pattern had begun. Two years later Wanda became pregnant again. Now they felt settled into a stable life-style that was both gratifying and creative. Phil now held a high administrative job. Wanda had become active in local politics.

When their son entered kindergarten, Wanda experienced a depression and emptiness that she had not felt before in her life. With the three children in school and a housekeeper to run the house, Wanda had time and energy without a direction in which to channel them with real enthusiasm. She could go back to work, but secretarial work was no longer interesting to her. Since she found politics very exciting she decided to return to school for a degree in political science.

Wanda began going to school half time while becoming increasingly active in the political affairs of the community.

She was in the forefront of local opposition against industrialization of wilderness areas near the city.

Phil also became more community-minded and gave a great deal of his free time to community activities. He had become a vice president in his company and was increasingly influential in the community.

Over the years Phil and Wanda had found that many of their old friends who had continued to be oriented primarily to science and technological developments were no longer stimulating to them. Gradually they saw less of them as they became more involved in political and community activities.

During these years they had their share of misfortunes. Their home was destroyed by a brush fire, and the rebuilding was tedious, costly, and a severe strain on them emotionally. On one occasion Wanda had major surgery following a car accident which incapacitated her for several months. But none of this had the impact of Phil's heart attack. He was approaching fifty and, following his recovery, was advised to cut back his activities drastically. They decided that in order to conserve Phil's energies and limit his activities they would sell their home. They moved into a condominium apartment. Fortunately, Phil was able to continue his job but was advised by his physician not to add extra stressful activity to his daily routine. He also began to read a great deal in diverse fields—something he had always wanted to do but that had had a relatively low priority in the past.

Now Phil and Wanda appreciated their relationship more than ever. They blended well together, and neither felt crowded by the other. They had developed a life-style that changed through the years according to their own needs and circumstances. Each was able to continue his personal growth, and both were able to let go of whatever became obsolete in their life. When their children went off to college, they faced their most difficult letting-go of all, recognizing that the children were now adults, each independent from them in every way. Phil and Wanda adopted a more quiet life-style together, spending more of their spare time with each other.

Phil was fifty-five when he had a second and fatal heart attack. Wanda, of course, mourned deeply over her loss. Phil had often told her that he hoped he would not be disabled because of his heart condition, and, indeed, he had led an active life to the end. Now Wanda faced the most difficult adjustment of her life. She continued to serve on various committees and advisory boards within the educational system and helped to establish a nonprofit preschool nursery. Like Phil, she had resolved long ago to continue an active, vigorous life-style.

Phil and Wanda had lived together in a mutually nourishing intimacy that was a mainstay of their evolving life-style. In addition their intimate relationship enhanced the ability of each to experience the growth and development of their separate selves.

The Essence of Intimacy

The fundamental ingredient in intimacy is openness. This applies both to our relationship with ourselves and to our relationships with other people. Openness toward ourselves means not only being willing but wanting to confront ourselves with who we are—even though at times such confrontations are painful. Ideally, when a person is intimate with himself, he has no thought, feeling or impulse that is unacceptable to his inner self. He is accepting toward every aspect of what he experiences and every manifestation of himself in his own intrapsychic life. This does not at all mean that he likes every aspect of his character and personality, and indeed he often sees his own growth as a process of playing up and developing certain qualities, attitudes and kinds of behavior while seeking to diminish others.

Intimate relating to ourselves means seeking full awareness of our inner self. What we choose to share with our Intimate Other as well as what we keep private is our personal choice. Openness leads to intimacy only when it is spontaneous.

Even in the most intimate relationship imaginable, each person, if he is sufficiently in touch with himself, is aware that he has limits to his willingness to share himself with his Intimate Other. He is aware of his need for privacy in many areas of his thinking, feeling and acting and is comfortable excluding the other from these areas of his self. For example, the following are parts of dialogues between Intimate Others clearly stating their needs for separateness and private space.

MARTY: In a way I look forward to your summer trips to your mother's. I like having the house all to myself and no one to think about but me.

NANCY: Call me modest, old-fashioned or whatever, I don't like to use the bathroom together.

PAULINE: For me your reassurance about my sexual anxieties seems superficial. Anyhow, after we talk about sex I usually feel worse. All I ever get from you in response is "book knowledge." So, it's true—I'd rather not bring it up with you. I'd rather talk to my sister about it.

DAN: I thought we had a clear understanding that the room over the garage is mine. I really resent finding my papers and books moved and rearranged. In that room I like things left where I put them. When it needs cleaning I'll do it.

SUSAN: Buzz off! My sex life before I met you is my business, and I intend to keep it that way. So stop your damn questioning!

Intimate relating reflects an attitude with which two people respond to each other. It is the quality of relating rather than a measurement of the degree of exposure of each self.

In intimate relating, there are no judgments by either person concerning what each "should" be willing to relate to or be open about. Rather, it is acknowledged that each person *must* feel free to be closed, withdrawn or turned off and that this is a prerequisite attitude within each self in order to feel fully free to be open when one so chooses. One recognizes one's own and the other's right to regulate his or her openness and self-expression in harmony with the needs of their separate selves.

PART TWO

TOXIC PATTERNS AND TOXIC MYTHS

5

TOXIC PATTERNS IN INTIMATE RELATING

TOXIC PAIRING

Many people relate to others with attitudes, motivations and methods that doom the relationship from the start. Toxic pairing refers to manipulative relationships in which one or both people are motivated primarily by anxiety or fear or seek to escape their insecurities by becoming involved in a relationship that they hope will remedy their inner dissatisfactions. The person is interested in the other not primarily as a person but rather as an object serving a purpose. In his efforts to manipulate another individual he may be aware of considerable tension as he squeezes himself in order to avoid revealing his deceptive motivations.

In toxic pairing the manipulation usually requires some kind of tactic or plan. To execute these manipulative programs, the person must maintain constant watchfulness to avoid any spontaneous emergence of self which might create suspicion or warn his prey that everything is not open and above board.

In toxic pairing the manipulator may not believe that he or she is being dishonest but may think that the pairing is the most effective way of becoming intimate and that, once intimacy is achieved, the record can then be set straight and the relationship put on a more honest basis.

Those who imagine they can achieve an intimate relationship through manipulative devices are living in a fantasy.

If we maintain a healthy reserve (this may include distrust or suspiciousness in spite of our embarrassment at harboring these feelings), particularly during the formative period of an intimate relationship, we can sharpen our awareness of potential toxic interaction. In this way we can avoid a great deal of unnecessary pain. At no time is an ounce of prevention better than a pound of cure than at the beginning of a relationship.

Gaining awareness of toxic patterns in our intimate relating means being willing to face the pain of disappointment or rejection when we discover that the relationship is not what we had hoped for.

The following contrasting nourishing and toxic attitudes are intended to enhance the reader's awareness of whether he or she fosters the development of toxic patterns or actively takes a stand against them.

1. **Nourishing:** Do I take responsibility for terminating a relationship that has remained for some time at a level that lacks the intimacy I want and wastes my time and energy?

   or

   Toxic: Do I continue to spend time in a relationship that lacks this degree of intimacy while hoping that somehow we will become more intimate?

2. **Nourishing:** Do I reach out to new people and actively seek someone with whom I feel a potential for developing an Intimacy of Two?

   or

   Toxic: Do I passively hope that someone with whom I can relate intimately will come into my life?

3. **Toxic:** Do I detour myself from real intimacy by becoming involved with someone who is interesting *but* unavailable, with an understanding that "we will keep it light"?

   or

   Nourishing: Am I willing to face the reality that this lessens my availability for other more meaningful relationships?

4. **Toxic:** Am I under the illusion that I can decide how involved I will become with another person and that I can control my emotional involvement the way I control a water faucet?

   or

   Nourishing: Am I aware that in intimate relating, emotional involvement cannot be regulated or programmed?

TOXIC AVOIDANCE

The obvious is frequently the last thing we are willing to see, especially when it carries an unwelcome message. Avoiding the obvious often means avoiding awareness of important toxic aspects of a relationship. We often poison ourselves with this avoidance. It lessens our chances of getting the kind of intimacy we *know* we need. Instead we may follow one blind-alley relationship after another—using up our lives in the process.

> JANE (*to her best friend, Mary*): I can't understand why Bill hasn't called. We had such a good time. Considering it was our first date, we really shared some intimate things with each other.
>
> MARY: Well, maybe he's been busy. You're probably not the only person in his life, you know. After all, it's only been two weeks.
>
> JANE: But he really seemed to like me, and I had a definite feeling that he wasn't involved with anyone else, and he said he would call me.

We often frustrate ourselves by trying to explain another person's behavior. When we try to psych out someone else (read his head), we not only engage in a self-poisoning process, we may also avoid giving our attention to other obvious aspects of our experience. In this example the simple fact is that Bill is ignoring Jane. He is making an obvious statement: He is not sufficiently interested to have contacted her. When Jane continues to ponder what's going on, she ignores the fact that Bill's not calling her for two weeks *is* an active decision.

The Message Is There

When we come to our senses (pay attention to the data from our sensory apparatus and intuitive feelings), we may become aware of the potential, or lack of it, for intimacy with a particular other person. By observing his behavior with other people and the way he relates to the world around him, we can learn to tune in on our own "vibes," which tell us what kind of relationship we might expect by involving ourselves intimately with a particular person.

> *Walter arrives at Terri's home for a blind date; Terri is recently divorced and has a four-year-old child. When Walter arrives Terri is ready, the babysitter is there and four-year-old Sharon is watching television. After introductions the following dialogue occurs:*

TERRI: Now be a good girl, Sharon, and do what Dianne (*the babysitter*) tells you.

SHARON: I don't want you to go. I want you to stay here with me. Why can't I go with you?

TERRI: Now let's not make a scene every time I go out. I've explained this to you before. Dianne will take care of you. You'll go to sleep in a while, and when you wake up, I'll be here.

SHARON: Last time I woke up and you weren't here.

DIANNE: Yes, last time she woke up about an hour after you left and wanted to know if you were back yet.

TERRI: Now listen, Sharon, you're getting old enough to understand this, and I don't want to go through this every time I go out. Now you behave yourself, and I don't want any more fussing.

(*Sharon, sitting on the floor with her head down, begins to weep quietly.*)

TERRI: I just can't stand you when you're like this. Dianne, take her in the other room and put her to bed, and if she doesn't stop crying in ten minutes give her something to cry for. We're leaving.

It is understandable that Terri might be anxious about her new date and embarrassed by Sharon's making a fuss, but she shows little willingness to comfort Sharon or spend a little time trying to reassure her. Her impatience and annoyance are indications of her lack of empathy.

As Walter and Terri drive to a restaurant, she tries to put this episode behind them, bringing up various topics. She is aware that Walter is uneasy and nervous. He has never been married and is obviously uncomfortable around women.

TERRI: Relax, Walter. You look nervous and tense. I'm not going to bite you.
WALTER: I'm usually a little up tight on my first date.
TERRI: I think that's cute.
(*They arrive at the restaurant, and Walter finds that although they have a reservation they will have to wait about ten minutes for their table.*)
TERRI: Tell them we are not going to wait. We had a reservation and we expect them to keep it.

Terri sends a clear message that she is either not interested or she is unaware of Walter's needs and anxieties. Walter is aware of his discomfort, but Terri has not really done anything to him. Yet her reactions to conflict and frustration clearly indicate what he can expect—if he is willing to pay attention to the obvious.

If we listen to our senses when we meet someone more often than not we can know within a matter of hours whether or not there is a potential for real intimacy.

Sometimes our most urgent need is for an Intimacy of Two. At other times we may be interested in multiple relationships and definitely not interested in any single commitment. Or we may be interested primarily in ourselves and in seeking inner growth or fulfillment of needs and goals that turn our attention inward, so that any kind of intimate relating to others is of little importance.

1. **Nourishing:** When I am interested in an Intimacy of Two, do I pay attention to the messages another sends about what kind of Intimacy, if any, he or she is interested in, *and* what kind of relationship he or she doesn't want?

   or

   Toxic: Am I so focused on my own need for a one-to-one intimacy that I avoid confronting myself with clear indications that the other is not interested in this kind of intimacy?

2. **Nourishing:** When I am interested in an Intimacy of Two, do I avoid relating to those who, because of their circumstances, life-style or other (usually obvious) reasons, are in all likelihood unavailable or uninterested in an enduring intimacy?

or

Toxic: Do I ignore such circumstances in the hope that if we develop an Intimacy of Two these "difficulties" will somehow be resolved or fade away?

Connie believed that Al was very much in love with her and remained with his wife only for the sake of his two children. He had often expressed to her his overwhelming guilt at the thought of divorcing his wife. To Al this meant abandoning his children almost as if he were never to see them again. Connie understood Al's pain and felt a great deal of empathy. There was little doubt that they loved each other and, were it not for these circumstances, would like nothing more than a mutual commitment to each other.

One day Al told Connie that his wife was pregnant. His explanation was that he felt so trapped through both his love and guilt toward his children that he might as well have a third child since he had always wanted three children.

Connie was devastated. A few weeks later she said good-bye to Al. She still loved him as much as ever, but she now realized that with his attitude and life situation she no longer could feel a reasonable hope that he would be available in the future as a potential Intimate Other.

Toxic relating and chronic loneliness go hand in hand and often reinforce each other in a vicious circle of frustration. The more painful a person's loneliness, the more liable he is to enter and remain in toxic relationships in the desperate belief that almost any relationship is preferable to the pain of loneliness. Pairing oneself off primarily to escape loneliness almost invariably results in a toxic relationship. Once the feeling of isolation diminishes, the person usually becomes increasingly bored or irritated yet remains unwilling to risk letting go because of the dread of returning to an empty existence. As long as this toxic stalemate remains, the quest for intimacy is stifled.

Frank and Hilda were in their late thirties when they met. Both had little dating experience, and neither had ever been intimately involved with anyone. Their initial meeting was unbelievably agonizing. Each was aware of his own and the other's shyness. Hilda was the first woman Frank had ever dated who seemed nonthreatening. He had always felt embarrassed going to a movie or a restaurant alone. Now he was comfortable with Hilda along and no longer felt that people were staring at him or wondering why he was alone. Hilda was mainly preoccupied with her fears that she would say or do the wrong thing and Frank would lose interest in her. She, too, saw a solution to her loneliness in their relationship.

They began having an affair, but real emotional intimacy between them was lacking. Both were too frightened to be open to the other. It could scarcely be said that they were in love; rather, they simply got used to each other. Their relationship was empty and sterile, but for each it seemed a good bargain to exchange for the bitter loneliness they had previously experienced.

After their marriage their life was more like that of roommates than anything approaching a love relationship. Their mutual fearfulness prevailed, and the stalemate solidified. Both grew increasingly angry and frustrated; yet neither would dare express such feelings except by further withdrawal. As the underlying tension continued, Hilda began to develop vague physical symptoms, which her physician reassured her were "just nerves." About the same time, Frank began to drink heavily, particularly on weekends. Now, after fourteen years of marriage, they live a routine life with their three children in a suburb of a large city. Each feels as empty as ever; yet neither has any inclination to change anything. Quiet desperation is the underlying tone of their life-style.

Choosing the Unavailable

This is another form of toxic avoidance, one that is closely allied to refusing to face the obvious.

Rex had lived the life of an adventurer, a political rebel, and had held several managerial positions. Although he had lived with various women, these relationships somehow never lasted more than a few months. Rex was aware that his relationships lacked stability but attributed this to his diverse interests and "restlessness."

Now, in his middle thirties, he began to feel an increasing depression at the limited depth of his relationships and his feeling of sameness about each woman with whom he became involved. When he met Eloise he began to feel that here was a person with whom he might commit himself to an enduring intimacy.

Early in their relationship Eloise told Rex about Carl, whom she cared for deeply but who was committed to work overseas for two more years. Rex only laughed at the idea of worrying about something two years in the future. Eloise reiterated that she wanted Rex to know about her other relationship before they became further involved. He continued seeing Eloise frequently, and his feelings for her grew far beyond his expectations. A year later he asked her to live with him. He had all but forgotten about Carl, and Eloise had not mentioned him again. When Eloise rejected his proposal Rex got angry.

"I've never felt like this toward anyone. I want to marry you, and you give me this crap about some guy you haven't even seen for two years."

Eloise remained steadfast about at least waiting until Carl returned and not making any commitment until then.

Circumstances often present realistic barriers to intimacy. When we are aware of the obvious complications that these existing realities may present, we often rationalize them away or otherwise dismiss them, so that they do not frustrate our present desires. This avoidance of the obvious may alleviate our anxiety in the immediate situation but is more apt to lead to a disastrous outcome at some future time. It is a kind of toxic "living for the moment" (in contrast to living *in* the moment) that expresses immaturity, impulsivity and unwillingness to accept the future consequences of present decisions.

T people frequently ignore such consequences by involving themselves in relationships despite an initial awareness that circumstances greatly diminish the likelihood of developing an enduring intimacy with a particular individual.

Don't Make Waves

Much toxic pain in intimate relationships stems from our refusal to face toxic patterns that we know have existed for some time. We avoid rocking the boat for fear that any confrontation would mean the end of the relationship. We cling to the hope that the destructive aspects will somehow go away if we ignore them.

T people often complain that they never seem to find nourishing people interested in an Intimacy of Two. That all the "good ones" are taken. Their failure to establish intimate relationships often reflects their lack of courage in confronting themselves with their own awareness that they are involved in a toxic relationship. Instead they use up their lives (weeks, months or years) hoping that somehow "things will change" if only they are patient enough, try harder and, above all, don't make any waves.

TOXIC "HELPFULNESS"

Margaret related to Chris as if he were part God. She felt almost privileged that he chose to be with her and listened to him as if he were a prophet. Early in their relationship Chris had decided to help her. His "help" turned out to be continually pointing out what she was doing "wrong." She felt grateful to him for this and struggled valiantly to win his approval.

"I am just amazed at his patience with me. He calmly keeps pointing out my failures to me even though I don't seem to be improving."

Despite her gratitude for Chris's tolerance, Margaret became aware of a feeling of desperation within her. While she and Chris were not living together, they had been with each other almost daily for many months. Finally Margaret confronted herself with a persistently gnawing awareness that, when she did not see Chris on a particular day, she felt a definite sense of relief. Subsequent to this self-confrontation she became increasingly aware of how tense she felt when she was with Chris. Her efforts to "prove herself" were exhausting. The toxic quality of their relationship (despite Chris's good intentions) became increasingly apparent to her. Now she felt intensely resentful of his attempts to be helpful (criticisms). Her last words to him, as she ended the relationship, were: "Go preach to someone else. I've had enough of your helpfulness."

Regardless of our caring for others, we cannot do their growing for them. Nor can anyone else do our growing for us. Growth is a process that emerges from within the self. Helpfulness usually turns out to be a toxic intrusion. The helper tries to persuade, cajole or in other ways "sell" some thing, or make the other person feel guilty if the other person insists on doing things his or her own way.

When we are interested in the growth of an Intimate Other, the most effective way of expressing this, as well as avoiding toxic games of being "helpful," is to stand out of the way and not impede the experimentation and self-initiating processes of the other person.

When we have suggestions that "work," the Other may appreciate our assistance. And we may solve their immediate conflict or alleviate their pain. The toxic effect comes from depriving them of the opportunity to initiate and experiment with their own solutions. In this way we hamper their potential growth. The more "successful" we are in coming up with good ideas and "workable answers" to the problems of our Intimate Other, the more we teach them to be dependent on us and in that way stifle their growth. In the long run the victim is apt to resent the other for his or her superior ability—and in addition resent his or her own continued feelings of inadequacy or helplessness.

I Have a Right to Know What's Going On With You

Good intentions in relating are commonly experienced in an Intimacy of Two through well-meant questions about what's going on with the other person.

Questioning carries an implicit message to the other
that it is not all right to remain silent.

Questioning intrudes on the integrity of the other person
and his freedom to initiate his relating on the basis of his
own needs for self-expression and contact.

> *Betty and Ed had just finished making love, and for
> Betty it had been an unusually intense experience. While
> they were still holding each other tightly, Betty began
> gently sobbing and holding Ed even tighter. She con-
> tinued to cry for a moment or two while Ed became in-
> creasingly tense and anxious. The following dialogue then
> occurred:*
> ED: What's the matter? Why are you crying? Did I do
> something wrong?
> BETTY: Ed, you're beautiful and I love you. Let's not talk
> for a while.
> ED: I don't understand why you're crying, and I feel upset.
> Is there something you don't want to tell me?
> BETTY: I'll talk about it later, Ed, please.
> ED: What kind of relationship do we have anyway? Here
> we've just been so close, making love and everything, and
> now you shut me out.

Although Ed's anxiety and interest in knowing what's
going on with Betty were legitimate, his questions were
obviously intrusive to her. Instead of being aware of this
and not pressing her to explain herself, Ed is preoccupied
with his need to alleviate his anxiety, at Betty's expense. In

so doing he takes away her freedom to be open and expressive as she chooses. As time goes on Betty becomes increasingly hesitant to express her emotions nonverbally. The inhibiting effect of Ed's questions lessen her sexual enjoyment and in turn make sex less exciting for Ed as well.

TOXIC PROJECTION

Dialogues between couples are toxic when one person assumes the role of critic or judge even under the guise of helpfulness.

Usually the critic projects unacceptable parts of himself onto the other. When he has an unpleasant feeling, he attributes it to the other person and blames the other for his bad feeling. Or he may avoid his own feelings of inadequacies or helplessness by pushing the other person to excel, work harder, expand his potentials.

Whatever we want to change in someone else is a reflection of a lack of full acceptance of ourselves. This is the mechanism of projection. Its toxic power on intimate relating can scarcely be overemphasized.

The Loving Helpmate: A Case History of Toxic Projection

CINDY (*driving home with her husband from a party at his boss's home*): You really embarrassed me—sitting in the corner acting as if you weren't interested in anybody and scarcely saying anything.

HARRY: I'm surprised to hear you say that. I was very interested in the conversation and was enjoying myself.

CINDY: Well, I thought you were bored. Sitting there as if you didn't have a thought in your head. Your boss was comparing you to the other men. I was watching him, and he felt embarrassed for you.

HARRY: I just didn't have much to say, and I'm not interested in trying to impress people. I never claimed to be the life of the party.

CINDY: I'm upset because I care about you. I know you're ambitious, and I'm trying to help you to see how you might get ahead faster.

HARRY: I'm not as ambitious as you think.

CINDY: What's that supposed to mean?

HARRY: I want to do a good job, but I'm not going to work at it when we're out socially and that includes when we're at my boss's house.

CINDY: You're unrealistic. You were always a dreamer. If you really want to get ahead, you use every opportunity to impress the right people.

HARRY: That's probably true, and I'm not *that* ambitious.

CINDY: Well, that's where you need me. I'm not so ambitious that I want you to do something you don't want to do, but you have to remember that there are a lot of people who would like your job. Sometimes I feel I have to be ambitious enough for both of us.

Cindy may have good intentions, but her attitude toward Harry is one of trying to get him to be as ambitious as *she* is. Rather than owning this need as a part of herself, she projects her ambition onto her husband and then tries to convince him that what *she* wants is also what he wants.

The following is a more nourishing dialogue about the same situation:

> CINDY: I wish you had had more to say tonight. The other men were really playing up to your boss. I worried that they would get the promotions, not you.
> HARRY: Yes, some of them were working pretty hard. I didn't feel like doing that.
> CINDY: Perhaps I'm overly ambitious. I don't mean to be pushing you.

Double Projection: Mutual Fingerpointing

Another form of toxic projection occurs when both people play one-upmanship games, whether by boosting their own self above the other or by attempting to put the other down as if each is struggling to score the most points. They relate as antagonists, which always means that no matter who wins the immediate point, they both lose in the long run.

The Attack Dialogue

> HE: I don't like your rejecting me.
> SHE: I don't like your making me feel guilty when you feel rejected.
> HE: Don't put your guilt trip on me. That's yours.

SHE: If you didn't act like a baby, I wouldn't have to feel guilty.

HE: You just can't let me be where I am, can you?

SHE: Would you like to try that one on for size and see if it fits you?

This is the initial phase of a typical dialogue between two chronic bickerers which only leads to further toxic interaction as each dumps his problem on the other.

Nolan and Kim are having a series of consultations with a psychologist regarding their problem in communicating. They are both strong, capable people. Nolan is aware of his dominant role in the relationship. He senses that Kim is more threatened by their conflicts and apprehensive about being outspoken for fear that this will irritate Nolan all the more.

KIM: I find it hard to talk to you. I'm afraid you'll get angry with me. Sometimes I feel frightened of you.

NOLAN: I'm going to say what I have to say, and if you're frightened that's your problem. Nobody is going to tell me when to stop talking.

KIM: I'm not trying to tell you to stop talking. What I'm saying is that you make your point and you keep building it up and making it into something bigger and bigger and I get scared when you make big issues out of little things.

NOLAN: They're little things to you. They're not little things to me. Nobody is going to make me shut up.

KIM (*starting to get angry*): I'm not telling you to shut up; I'm telling you to get off my back. You keep going over the same thing, beating the same dead horse. Even when I agree with you, you still keep hammering away at the same point. What do you want from me?

NOLAN: I want to show you that I'll finish talking when I'm done, not when you want me to be done.

KIM: I run out of patience trying to sit here and listen to you repeat yourself until you feel finished.

NOLAN: Well, I suggest you try to be more patient, then.

KIM: Don't tell me what to do!

NOLAN: Then don't tell me to shut up!

KIM: You just like to fight. Especially when you feel you're winning.

NOLAN: Yes, I do like to fight, and when I think you're wrong about something I really like to press it home to make sure you see how wrong you are.

In this dialogue what Nolan is really saying is that *he* feels ineffective and doesn't believe that anybody listens to him. Rather than confront himself with his own feelings of ineffectiveness, he projects them onto Kim by insisting that he is simply maintaining his right of self-expression by not allowing her to shut him up.

The main projection on Kim's part is her fear of Nolan, which she expresses by squeezing her self and trying to be patient. Underneath her patience and quietness, she is really frightened by her own anger at Nolan's repetitiousness. When she is in touch with her anger, Kim is quite aware that what she would like to do *is* to tell him to shut up or even to leave the room if he won't shut up. She is afraid to do this for fear that Nolan would be more angry if she left the room and in this way succeeded in shutting him up.

Intimacy versus "Shoulds"

To the degree that a relationship is based on duty, obligation or other coercions, the potential for an enduring intimate relationship is hampered. Duty and obligation are external rules, and "shoulds" that are forced on us and usurp our right to determine various aspects of a relationship for ourselves. The wantingness and willingness of each person are then superseded by these external regulations. It is idealistic to hope that two people can relate in a purely spontaneous fashion in an ongoing intimate relationship. Yet the opposite extreme, a relationship based largely on duty and obligation, is toxic and destroys the chances of sustaining real intimacy.

Choosing to relate on an intimate level means giving up the external "shoulds" and other manipulations intended to force ourselves and others to act out of duty and obligation. To the degree that we demand that the other do his duty or meet his obligation, we eliminate the potential intimacy in the relationship.

TOXIC GAMES

Frequently people are frightened that their anger threatens to destroy their relationship totally. A T person often compromises his integrity in order to avoid angry outbursts: "I'll give you what you want—just don't explode." In this way he becomes an easy prey who can be manipulated whenever the other feels frustrated and wants his own way. The victim in this game adopts a "peace at any price" attitude to buy the other off in order to avoid an angry outburst.

Watch Out, or I'll Blow My Stack!

SAM: How could you go ahead and buy that sewing machine without my permission?

SARAH: I've been asking you for two years to buy me a sewing machine, and you keep telling me, "Not now." I told you my old machine cannot be repaired, and I have enjoyed sewing ever since we were married, and that's been twenty-two years, in case you've forgotten.

SAM: How do you like that? I work my ass off all day, and you go out and spend my money on your hobbies.

SARAH: But Sam, you know how much money I save making clothes. Even the shirt you're wearing I made myself.

SAM: There you go. Now I suppose you're going to tell me you bought the sewing machine as a favor to me. (*Sam starts to get red in the face and is breathing heavily.*) I just can't stand it when you spend money without my permission. (*He starts to pound his fist on the table.*)

SARAH: Well, you won't let me go to work. What am I supposed to do when I want something? You tell me a woman's place is in the home, with the kids.

SAM: I could really smash you. You make me so angry. No matter what I say, you always have an argument. (*Sam is now shouting, pacing up and down, while Sarah is getting increasingly nervous and begins to bite her fingernails.*)

SARAH: All right, all right, I'll take it back. I didn't mean to upset you. You get mad at me every time I bring it up. You tell me I'm nagging at you. Forget it. I'll take the machine back.

SAM: Why do I have to get angry before you get sensible? Be sure you take it back first thing in the morning, and I want to see the receipt.

Two months later:

SARAH (*as Sam walks in the door after a hard day's work*): Sam, I know you're going to get mad, and I know it was terribly stupid of me, but I scratched the fender on our new car when I was backing out of the garage this morning.

Seldom in an ongoing relationship does a person really surrender to another. A domineering person like Sam may *appear* to control Sarah completely, she seems so passive, compliant and conscientious in trying to please Sam (an impossible task!). Yet, somehow—even after being married to him for twenty-two years—she "forgets" the little things she knows will aggravate him or has "accidents" with his prized possessions.

Dominating and controlling one's Intimate Other is a "top dog" game. The top dog seems to overpower the other one, the "underdog." Almost invariably the weaker, intimidated underdog learns to be clever (consciously or unconsciously) and usually wins by subtly sabotaging the needs and plans of the top dog.

Men Are Chauvinist Pigs, and Women are Castrating Bitches

It is toxic to carry social issues into our personal relating to others with whom we seek intimacy. A woman may resent the subservient position to which she has been relegated by society, past or present. A man may resent the loss of his traditional role of "Lord and Master" of the household.

An Intimacy of Two is *primarily* a relationship between two people; whether one is male and one is female or whether both are of the same sex is irrelevant. Nourishing people do not experience their Intimate Other primarily in terms of sex gender.

Milford had inherited his father's paperhanging business and, like his father, was a skilled craftsman who always had more work than he could handle. On weekends he liked to relax around the house, do a little gardening, take his family on an outing or visit friends. For a long time there were recurring arguments between Milford and his wife, Laurie, when he would refuse to repair things around the house.

MILFORD: I work all week, and I like to relax and do other things on the weekend.

LAURIE: But these things only take you a minute, and I hate to spend our money to hire someone.

MILFORD: When I work I make three times as much as any handyman.

LAURIE: That's not the point. You're here—all you're doing is watching television. Sometimes you act like you're just too good for this kind of work.

MILFORD: If I have to work on weekends I would rather hang paper.

LAURIE: You men, with your superior attitude! I guess what I do here, raising the kids and taking care of the house, isn't worth much either!

MILFORD: You women! A man works his tail off, and all you do is bitch! You take your days off during the week. The weekend is my free time.

LAURIE: You're a typical male chauvinist after all!

Laurie and Milford obviously have a conflict of interests and have yet to find a resolution acceptable to both. However, in this dialogue they are playing a "win/lose" game in which their attitudes are those of antagonists rather than a constructive approach to resolving their problem together. Nourishing communicating is lost when we become angry and attack our Intimate Other with social generalizations and clichés about the other's sex role.

It is always toxic to intimate relating when we criticize through any reference to another person's sex, politics, occupation or group identification of any kind.

As we begin to recognize toxic patterns within ourselves or in our relationship with an Intimate Other, we can replace them with more-nourishing patterns and thus become even more intimate with our inner self as well as with our Intimate Other. Many toxic patterns are so obvious that once we recognize them, it is hard to understand why we did not recognize them earlier. We need not blame ourselves for this. The fact of recognition is, instead, to be welcomed as a sign of growth.

Greediness Is Toxic

Instead of appreciating what is given to us in our intimacy with another, we may contaminate this nourishment with our expectations and demands for more. Instead of appreciating the nourishment we receive from an Intimate Other and responding in turn with care and givingness, we too often try to manipulate, cajole or coerce the other into giving more. This kind of toxic manipulation overtaxes the other and, in addition, destroys the spontaneity of giving and being intimate.

Competition Is Toxic

In an Intimacy of Two competition, an antagonism that involves a struggle of one against the other is poisonous to their intimacy. Such struggles of one against the other usually involve needs that the other is not willing to meet. That person's refusal to respond to the needs of the other is not acceptable to the other, i.e., the unwillingness is considered invalid. The needy other then attempts to get through battle and other forms of manipulation what was not willingly given.

Intimacy Is Not Easy

Although the process of developing and sustaining a growing Intimacy of Two is not easy, we make it many times more difficult by wasting time and energy trying one quick solution or gimmick after another.

As each new gimmick, technique or "we'll make it easy for you" program fails, as they inevitably do, to live up to its tantalizing promise, many people begin to believe that they lack the ability to relate or that the task is just too difficult. They tend to feel that their failure reflects some lack within themselves. They are unaware that they are looking in the wrong places for the solutions to their need for intimacy.

TOXIC ISOLATION

Some people, despite superficial appearances to the contrary, are basically out of contact with others and relate to the world with an almost wholly self-centered attitude. They remain psychologically alone and without any real emotional connection to those they seemingly care for and have a relationship with. Instead they manifest a basic lack of respect for the integrity and needs of others. To relate to such people means essentially to do everything their way. This kind of one-way-street relating will, of course, kill the growth and stability of any really intimate relationship.

The Toxic Loner

At first the toxic loner simply appears to have high standards of performance and a rigid attitude about how to do things. Often he has the status and material trimmings of the successful achiever. In work he is efficient and gets things done. Yet his rigid way of doing things, his intolerance of differences between himself and his Intimate Other, present a most difficult dilemma. Often he does everything well (or he wouldn't do it at all) and uses his talents to manipulate the other person into feeling inadequate and second-rate.

Ben and Lana have been going together about two months and are considering living together. Both are excited about the possibilities of their relationship.

BEN: I'm looking forward to spending weekends together skiing. I'll teach you everything I know about it. I want you to be good at it.

LANA (*sensing Ben's expectations*): Yes, I love skiing—only I hope I don't disappoint you.

BEN: You've got a natural athletic aptitude. You'll learn quickly. You'll see.

LANA: I hope so. I'm often afraid you'll decide I'm not enough for you.

(*Ben starts to fix dinner, which he always insists on doing. Among his achievements, he is a fantastic cook, and Lana recognizes his superiority in this area too.*)

LANA: Is there anything I can do to help?

BEN: Yes. Would you stir the sauce while I fix the vegetables, and be sure not to let it boil.

LANA: Love to.

(*Five minutes later Ben walks over to see how the sauce is coming.*)

BEN: Jesus Christ! You let the sauce get stuck on the bottom. Don't you know you have to stir it deeply, not just on the surface? Go in the living room and sit down. I'll finish the whole thing myself.

In this minor incident is a message of the kind of toxic-wipe-out Lana can continue to expect from Ben. She can never be sure that what she is doing is to his satisfaction. This is the toxic loner in operation. His intolerance for differences, least of all inefficiencies, makes intimate relating almost impossible. There is a particular sadness about this kind of interaction, since the victim not only may have deep feelings of love for the other but a genuine appreciation of his talents and abilities.

The possibilities of nourishment through relating with an Intimate Other are endless.

It is a self-induced toxic attitude when we decide to give up or consider ourselves ineligible for an Intimacy of Two.

Many of us surrender our potential ability to find new intimacies when we surrender to any of the following three widely accepted toxic fantasies, each of which reflects a lack of understanding of the meaning of an Intimacy of Two.

First, many people poison themselves by insisting that age somehow disqualifies them from intimacy. The stereotyped picture of an Intimacy of Two in our culture often implies that this is a more or less exclusive option of young adults. Or, at least, that it must begin during this period of our lives.

The second toxic attitude occurs when we evaluate our chances for intimacy on the basis of sexual attractiveness.

Lastly, we can poison ourselves by making conclusions based on past performance; i.e., we can believe that each past "failure" in intimate relating lessens our chances and even abrogates our right to continue pursuing this kind of relationship. This is expressed by some people who have "failed" in a marriage and become resolute that their next marriage will work. If the second marriage fails their plight is even more desperate, and their grim determination and resolution not to make further mistakes simply sets the stage for all kinds of toxic patterns that make future "failures" even more likely.

Using any or all of these toxic "excuses," countless numbers of people poison themselves by concluding that there is something wrong with them and they might just as well give up the pursuit of intimacy regardless of how badly they may wish it.

The ultimate cop-out is when we ignore the reality that each of us is evolving and changing, that intimacy is always possible regardless of one's past experiences. It is toxic to believe that the past dictates a similar outcome in the present or future.

6

TOXIC MYTHS ABOUT INTIMACY

Our culture perpetuates many irrational myths that poison us with expectations about how we *should* think, feel and act in our intimate relationships. Toxic myths, for instance, often portray intimacy between two people as an enchanting fairy tale that we then seek to achieve in reality. The power of these myths is enhanced by the assumption that others actually experience this fairy-tale fulfillment. This makes us feel that we, too, have a right to expect or at least hope for this same enchantment. For example, an aura of magic is often placed around a romance between glamorous celebrities like Elizabeth Taylor and Richard Burton. Thousands of words are written that foster our romantic illusions. When our experiences fail (as they inevitably do) to live up to these fantasies, we often poison ourselves with feelings that we are either inadequate or lacking in some way or the world has been unfair to us.

Such toxic myths burden people with attitudes that hamper or even destroy the kind of self-acceptance necessary for an intimate, loving attitude toward ourselves. They also contaminate our intimate relating to others with their unnatural demands and expectations.

While most of us realize that all human beings experience similar joy and pain, hope and anxiety, cultural attitudes have a far more powerful effect on our personal lives than most of us are aware of or are willing to admit. In an Intimacy of Two, these toxic myths with their "shoulds," expectations and demands disrupt intimacy and lead to feelings of futility and despair.

To evaluate ourselves and our relationship with our Intimate Other in the light of these myths is to play a toxic comparison game. ("How well am I doing compared with how I should be doing?" "How well are we doing compared with the Joneses?")

The child is an easy victim of toxic myths that often burden him for the rest of his life. Stereotyped toys indoctrinate girls and boys with a host of unrealistic expectations. When has anyone seen an "unattractive" mass-produced doll? Dolls are always beautiful from head to foot. Soldiers are invariably handsome. Physical beauty is presented as the *sine qua non* of being lovable, so that the child who feels he is homely or unattractive—or who actually has some physical impairment—considers himself less than capable of loving and being loved, even less acceptable as a person. These "beauty myths" encourage us to devote unreasonable amounts of time and energy to enhancing our physical beauty. They encourage us to believe that the older we are the less chance we have for intimacy; to believe that because at forty we do not have the youthful body that we had at twenty we are automatically less attractive to others and face only the dismal prospect of continuously diminishing chances for intimate relationships.

We live under the toxic illusion that youth enhances our chances for intimacy.

The Expectations of Intimacy: The Toxic Bill of Rights

Each generation continues to be sold the idea of "inalienable rights" concerning what it has coming. We continue to teach children that they have a right to expect to be loved, cared for and held secure throughout their adult life by someone who loves them. This is a cruelly toxic myth, more of a bill of goods than a bill of rights. The components are:

1. If you love me you will fill the gaps of my unmet needs. When I feel insecure I expect you to free me from whatever anxiety I am unable to cope with on my own. After all, what's a relationship for if I can't expect you to do things for me?
2. Once you tell me you love me, I have the right to various expectations. If you love me you are obligated to me in various ways. Our relationship is now different from what it was the moment before you declared your love. Now there are things you must do for me, especially if I ask them of you, that you were not obliged to do before. There are also things that you no longer have a right to do without my consent.
3. A declaration of love for another automatically means the surrender of one's individual freedom.

4. If you love me you are not supposed to reject me in any way.
5. You are not supposed to fall *out* of love. This is frowned on not because of the sadness of a lost relationship but because of the implication that falling out of love is a "bad," shameful thing for one person to do to another.
6. Emotions and feelings are like water flowing from a faucet and can be turned on and off if the person really wants to. If you stop loving me you are being cruel and hurtful.
7. Intimacy equals Permanency, and Permanency means that an Intimate Relationship exists. The poetry and prose of our culture is filled with promises of "foreverness," as if one has a right to view an intimate love relationship as a permanent, unalterable state.

If we consider all the one-to-one relationships beginning in the teens and continuing throughout one's life, those that are permanent probably amount to fewer than one in a hundred. Most people have been involved in a number of intimate relationships in which they eventually rejected the other person or were rejected. Yet toxic myths continue to poison us with the notion that permanency is an implicit right once we are intimately involved and in love.

"Dating Is a Pain in the Ass"

Dating should be fun—according to the all-pervasive folk myth—yet for many people dating, regardless of age, is often a laborious process of making contact with others and continually weeding out unacceptable partners. Most dating is superficial relating, sexually or otherwise, after which the relationship terminates. It is primarily an experimental shopping for others with whom one may sense the excitement and potential for a deeper intimacy. Such experiences are bound to be frustrating, since they usually imply a continuing deprivation of intimacy. Many people actually react to random dating with feelings of depression, futility and cynicism. When an intimate relationship ends against our wishes, we often feel similar reactions, and the anticipation of renewing the search for new intimacy deepens these feelings. In reality, dating is a selective process that includes many negative and rejecting experiences. Yet the cultural myth insists that we are supposed to enjoy ourselves—to feel pleasant and cheerful and act as if we were having fun.

The following dialogue took place in a group therapy session:

DON (*age twenty-eight*): I'm really in touch with the fact that I sound like I'm in high school. I feel like my dates, my relationships, with women are on a par with a high school junior.

THERAPIST: Can you describe what that kind of date is for you?

DON: You meet someone in the class, and they're nice and cute. You go to a dance or some place, and you talk and joke and try to be really funny so she'll like you. If she likes you you can go and neck and you might even get laid. And you do all of that and get home before two A.M.! (*Laughter*)

And the next week you do the same thing. So that's what it's like for me, except that it's ten years later. I just feel . . . like an idiot, a shallow, superficial person. I keep doing it over and over again, and . . . it's really a depressing thing, and I feel depressed about it. So then I'll back away from it for a while, and then I'll go ahead and start it over . . . and it never gets better.

THERAPIST: What's the "it"?

DON: Confronting the situation of going through this very shallow cycle.

GEORGE: I'm sure identifying with you, and I felt the same way you do. I didn't want to have a relationship with a girl unless it was serious and meaningful, but I found out that I had to meet an awful lot of people before I found one that was going to turn into a meaningful relationship. I've been doing it all my life, off and on, and I hate to tell you, but I'm forty-seven!

DON: I really feel the need, and I really relate to the feeling of wanting to be married and have kids—the whole family life routine. And yet sometimes I'm a completely different person . . . I look at that and it scares me. Every friend I've got is divorced or married twice or something, and I think, "Wow, it doesn't have a chance!" And then I turn around, and I see somebody that I don't know very well, that's got three kids and they look really happy, and I think, "Boy, I really relate to all that!" (*Turning to George*) And you're forty-seven?

THERAPIST: How do you feel about George being forty-seven and doing the same thing?

DON: I feel in a way . . . it scares me. Here he is forty-seven, and he's doing what I'm doing . . . that scares me.

GEORGE: In high school it was malts, and now it's booze, but it's really the same.

BILL: You know, Don, you're expressing deep feelings about relationships between men and women. To think that it's shallow of you not to be able to easily find someone you're willing to make a big, big investment with, is your own trip.

DON: I meet somebody, we really enjoy each other, and the first impression is great. I could go out with her once a week for four or five weeks and still maintain other relationships, and she wouldn't expect so much because she knows I'm spending time with others. But instead sometimes I'll see someone seven or eight nights straight, and so she's saying, "Wow, this guy really digs me!" And all of a sudden she'll never hear from me again!

BILL: Why are you taking so much responsibility? It's like you're putting the women down. Don't you believe that they have any responsibility? Any right to decide? Are you somehow in charge of these relationships?

DON: Well, I'm also fantasizing. I know how much it hurt me to really be hurt. So after seven or eight times, maybe it's not a big deal to them if I just don't call them again and that's the end of it. I know I have a habit of feeling responsible for other people. I guess I am wiping out my power . . . by taking this responsibility for everybody—that it's my job to see that the girl doesn't get hurt. That's what it boils down to. I guess dating is contact with a lot of other people and one is always dropping the other one, meeting some new people—that's what dating is.

JEAN: I'm always getting very excited about relationships. I meet someone, he's neat, and I think I'm in love with this person. And he's so terrific, and so marvelous, and the next time I go out with him I've already found something wrong and I'm convinced that we could never make it. So I don't see him any more.

DON: But like a lot of times there won't even be that much. They might be just all right, and I really don't want to sit home by myself and just do nothing or go out drinking with a bunch of guys. But it's a senseless basis for a relationship if I'm really not that interested to start with. You know, maybe I'm really programmed from way back when. I wasn't brought up this way. You're supposed to be nice to people. Well, is it being nice to somebody to go out with them when you really aren't that interested in going out with them but it's better than anything else you can think of doing, so what the hell, why not?

JEAN: Isn't it possible that they feel the same way about

you? Isn't it possible that they had a good time for two or three nights and then decided that you're a drag, too?

DON: I suppose. It's O.K. for them to do it. I can accept that. Maybe four or five times . . . it's not that big a deal to them, and it wasn't that big a deal to me so . . . I don't feel badly about that. It's when they care that I feel bad.

JEAN: I understand. I just want to say I'm really aware of how perfect you want to be. You're not willing to be where you are. You want things to work out perfectly, and if they don't, you're imperfect . . . and you shouldn't be imperfect.

DON: Something that I see happening over and over again —it's a pain. I'm willing to be responsible for a new approach. Maybe if I went to a church or a laundromat and met somebody there—maybe just because it started differently it would be better. . . .

(*Laughter*)

THERAPIST: Do you see how you're completely ignoring your *self* with what you're saying right now?

DON: Yes.

THERAPIST: You sound like in most of your relationships you know if you're really interested after a few hours of actual relating, but you don't listen to yourself. Instead you're busy with your programs and your anxiety—you don't want to hurt this girl; she didn't do anything to you . . .

DON: What I'm hearing is that I'm not giving myself a fair chance. That I'd have a better chance of having a more meaningful relationship regardless of the time period involved if I got out of my straitjacket.

THERAPIST: Exactly!

DON: So I get out of it by recognizing that I cannot be responsible for somebody else. And in a way I'm really insulting them by implying that they are not able to take care of themselves, that these women wear their hearts on their sleeves and I'm some cad that comes along and sweeps away their virginity. That sounds like a real 1890 version—and then I leave them.

THERAPIST: And they've never experienced this before, and they'll never experience it again. Your catastrophic fantasy sounds like you've ruined their lives.

HANK: My number is the "nice guy" who comes along and says, "Let's keep it light, we're just going to have fun, and nobody's going to get hurt, right?" And if they agree —that's the contract. And of course it doesn't work. And then one of us says, "Well now, remember we agreed we were just going to keep it light and nobody was going to get hurt?" It's irrelevant. It's just another program. For me, what it boils down to is this: When you're looking for an intimate relationship, dating is a pain in the ass. Period. And I don't see any way to clean that up. All these singles groups—I moan and groan about them, too—but I've got to go out and try to meet people. As soon as I connect, I'm gone. I leave that scene right away.

DON: I felt like I should be interested in what the girl wants from me because she really is nice and hasn't done anything to me.

THERAPIST: That's how you poison yourself with your program. When she wants something from you and you're not interested, that's the message—you know you don't want to give her what she wants—if you're willing to listen instead of judging yourself.

Toxic myths about the differences between the sexes date back to antiquity. In intimate relating, the power of these myths is most devastating when they emphasize the sex of an individual as the principal determinant of how he or she relates within his or her separate self as well as in intimate relating with others.

Toxic myths that make sexuality primary, grossly distort the fact that, first and foremost, each of us is a
human being.

Such myths set the stage for endless poisonous conflicts
about one's sexual role, about acceptable and unacceptable
actions and reactions to a vast range of attitudes, and about
patterns of interaction in which these myths sanction certain modes of behavior by each sex and discourage others.

The proverbial battle of the sexes typifies the power of
these toxic myths to create an inherently poisonous attitude
that a person's struggle for his own survival, growth and the
satisfaction of his needs includes a considerable measure of
combat with the opposite sex. In intimate relating between
two people these sexist attitudes contribute nothing but de-
structiveness to their relationship.

The supposed differences of attitudes and expectations
between men and women are mostly unrealistic, reflecting
obsolete cultural patterns. Stereotypes of what a woman is
supposed to be and what a man is supposed to be create
endless conflicts within the person and in the interaction
between the sexes.

When a boy is taught that a *real man* is domineering and
aggressive, he is given a burden, a duty he must fulfill in
order to feel socially accepted. To do this, he struggles
against other men in various ways, almost all of which are
toxic, to prove his masculinity. At the same time, any qualities that are considered feminine are frowned upon. He is
encouraged to suppress such feelings, attitudes or behavior.

He is taught that strength is the opposite of needing to be dependent, cared for and mothered. He really is taught to isolate and deny his emotions. Each of these toxic expectations is an added barrier in his quest for intimate relationships.

The role of the girl is similarly defined in a lopsided, obsolete fashion. She is still encouraged to be passive, submissive and nonaggressive in most sections of this country. The culture at best tolerates her adventurousness, while clearly approving of her interests in marriage, children and domestic activities. Her eventual role as a mother is still placed so overwhelmingly in the forefront of these cultural expectations toward (against) her, that her individuality is usurped on the basis of her gender.

The rebellion against these stereotyped roles is obvious on many levels of our culture today. Perhaps the last area in which these changes will occur is in intimate one-to-one relating.

Nowhere are these toxic myths more destructive than in one's intimate life. They create nothing but direct animosity, resentment and conflict. They are the opposite of the essential prerequisite for any real intimate relationship—that the two people relate to each other primarily as individual human beings and that their gender is clearly subordinate.

---

*Love Is the Key to Happiness: Warning! This Myth Is
Deadly*

Toxic myths about love strongly suggest that our best
chance for happiness depends on finding someone to love.
The myth that love conquers all dominates the attitude of
many who search for a meaningful life. Like other toxic
myths, this one encourages us to live our lives with a re-
stricted, narrow view of reality. We blind ourselves to the
reality that life has many dimensions that are not inter-
changeable one for the other. A man who is thirsty may
have an abundance of food on which he can gorge himself,
but if he doesn't know what his need requires, he may be
bewildered that his thirst continues.

Harry had always been a restless person. After college
he spent two years drifting from one place to another,
searching for what he wanted. He returned home when his
father died and left the family business to him. He had very
little interest in the business but liked the generous income
it provided. When he met Colleen she was a rising starlet,
charming, intelligent and vivacious. They became increasingly intimate, but Harry continued compulsively seeking
new adventures. Almost in desperation he proposed to
Colleen, convincing her that they could build their love into
a stable, lasting life-style. Soon after the wedding, Harry
realized that marriage was not the answer either. His restlessness continued. He and Colleen decided to have a baby,
and for a while Harry felt more settled. He turned with
new interest toward his business, making more money than
ever and spending more time at the office. Colleen seemed
satisfied, particularly when their second child came. Between her acting career and her family, she felt her life was
full. She and Harry loved each other. To their friends their

life-style and relationship seemed ideal. Yet Harry was aware that the restless feeling that had always gnawed at him was again growing stronger. In desperation he had several love affairs. Finally he began to recognize that loving relationships even combined with material wealth and success did not provide the meaningfulness and contentment he had sought all of his life.

Again in the desperation that propelled him into each new situation, he decided to try psychotherapy. This helped him gradually become aware that his chronic restlessness was a way of avoiding his inner fears, anxieties and insecurities. With a new willingness to risk exploring his inner self, he began to experience a growing inner intimacy and self-love. He began to feel more whole and no longer needed to depend so completely for his well-being on the world around him and on those he loved. He no longer needed to burden them with the hopeless task of filling *his inner emptiness,* which until now he had found too frightening to face.

Oh, Where—Oh, Where Can My True Love Be?

The "Prince Charming" myth continues—in updated versions—to be widely believed. It implies not only that somewhere there is one particular person who was "meant for me" but also that fate alone will determine whether or not we ever find our true love. Our true love, according to this myth, will appear at the right time and place "if it is meant to be." The real poisonous effect of this attitude stems from what it implies—that fate determines our destiny. It encourages a passive, inactive role in the quest for intimate relationships, rather than an aggressive search.

A person involved in an Intimacy of Two may appreciate

the uniqueness of the other person, and he is usually aware of the loss he would feel if the relationship ended. This attitude is toxic, however, when it leads the person to conclude that he will never finish mourning his loss and that he will never again experience such intimacy with someone else. Of all the toxic myths about love and romance, this is one of the most destructive. It generates a sense of finality should the relationship end. It enhances feelings of futility which in extreme instances are manifested by an attitude that "my life is over." After all, according to such myths, how can there be more than one Prince (or Princess) Charming?

". . . and They Lived Happily Ever After"

The vast majority of one-to-one relationships are terminated by the free choice of one or both of the people involved. Or a relationship may continue but gradually deteriorate to the point that genuine intimate relating no longer exists. From the beginning of dating in adolescence and continuing throughout adulthood, people seek and experience intimate emotional involvement, only to find that such relationships deteriorate or end. Toxic myths encourage us to feel that such an outcome is unfair. This becomes a way of avoiding responsibility for the toxic patterns that contribute to the deterioration of intimate relationships.

Deeply embedded in our mythology of romance is the notion that it is reasonable to expect to find our "true love" and, once having found it, to remain in a state of bliss "till death do us part." This notion violates the reality of human experience. It encourages unrealistic expectations. Permanent love relationships between adults are the exception rather than the rule.

Our culture has a bias that relationships not based on love are somehow to be frowned upon. Toxic myths about romantic love encourage us to believe that if a person continues a relationship because he likes the life-style, material security or other creature comforts it offers, somehow he is dishonest if not downright deceptive.

Peggy, an extremely attractive woman, had been in love with love since she was thirteen. She read one romantic novel after another, each time falling in love with the male hero. Her expectations about men and love sounded like a movie script. It was not surprising that she always felt disappointed with the men she dated; they did not, of course, match her fantasies.

Peggy was twenty-five when she took a job as a private secretary to the owner of a small business. Mark, an aggressive, handsome man in his early thirties, was married and had children. Peggy admired his strength and maturity. He represented her ideal man. In her fantasies she concluded that his wife must be ecstatic married to him. It was quite a shock when one day Mark began talking to her about his marital problems. How could her hero have such commonplace domestic difficulties?

Occasionally, Peggy and Mark worked late and had dinner together afterward. Peggy began to feel guilt-ridden as she became more attracted to him. Her fantasies of an emotionally overwhelming sexual relationship became increasingly intense. Their affair began when Mark's wife learned that her mother was critically ill and flew to her side. Mark took the children to his sister's house to stay until his wife returned. When Peggy invited him for dinner at her apartment, he stayed the night. The evening began like one of

Peggy's favorite movies. There was a bottle of champagne and quiet music in the background. But it ended disastrously. Mark was impotent. He was embarrassed and explained apologetically that this was his first extramarital affair. In her desperate disappointment Peggy hardly heard his words. After Mark fell asleep, she wept quietly for hours. In the morning after Mark left she wrote him a letter resigning from her job. This was the first of a series of shattering experiences for Peggy.

She became anxious to reassure herself that she was sexually attractive. She had blamed Mark's impotency on herself. A few months later she began an affair with Bill, a man who cared about her and sensed her anxiety. She had no complaints about his lovemaking, but sex was far less gratifying than she had expected. The affair continued for several months, and Peggy found she could reach orgasm only when Bill stimulated her clitoris manually. He encouraged her to enjoy herself and said that perhaps in time she would reach a climax during intercourse. However, Peggy became increasingly obsessed about her lack of sexual responsiveness, which spoiled the sexual pleasure she did experience. She was a victim of the romantic myths and expectations she still clung to from her childhood.

Bill gradually became irritated and resentful. He began to avoid initiating sex. "I'm getting tired of our sex life being one big performance test" was his response when Peggy asked if he was losing interest in her. Now their quarrels were more frequent and more intense. Bill had told Peggy over and over that he loved her. Part of her romantic fantasy was that this meant she could take his love for granted, so it was a shock when Bill finally told her he wanted to end their relationship, that he no longer loved her. Peggy was outraged and bewildered, disillusioned and betrayed. Her romantic fantasies, which were so deeply ingrained, left her totally unprepared to cope with rejection.

She withdrew into a bitter isolation bemoaning her fate, insisting that Bill had ruined her life and angrily denouncing all men as liars.

Romantic myths portray the rejected lover as a helpless, pitiful victim who faces a tragedy that is not only unfortunate but downright unfair.

The man who rejects a woman is a bastard; the woman who rejects a man is a bitch. In the face of rejection these toxic myths make letting go of a relationship infinitely more difficult.

7

MULTIPLE RELATIONSHIPS: THE AVOIDANCE OF INTIMACY

Those who prefer multiple relationships are interested in and available for intimate relationships with a number of other people. What is lacking in these relationships, however, are the qualities of exclusiveness and mutual commitment as well as a primary interest in sustaining any one of these relationships.

This way of relating is summarized in the expression:

> I do my thing, you do your thing.
> We are together as long as it's beautiful.
> If not, it can't be helped.

In multiple relationships there is relatively little dissonance or conflict, since each person continues the relationship and the sharing of experiences with another person only as long as this process is easy and no significant inter-personal obstacles present themselves. When important differences do occur, the two people simply disengage and turn to others. In a multiple relationship pattern the individuals with whom a person is involved are far more readily replaceable than in one-to-one relating. Multiple relationships are intrinsically different from one-to-one intimacy. They are contradictory. For example, multiple relating implies that sexual gratification can be enjoyed without leading to an increasing emotional involvement or a desire by one or both people for an exclusive, one-to-one relationship.

It is fantasy to expect that when we seek intimate relating we can separate our sexual needs from our need to relate to others in a more fulfilling manner.

Open marriage (another popular term for multiple relationships) suggests that avoiding the restrictions of commitment actually enhances a one-to-one intimacy. Marriage in any meaningful (not legal) sense of the word means some kind of commitment between two people in which they consent to restrict their relationships with others in certain ways. In this sense, multiple relationships stand in marked contrast to an Intimacy of Two.

In discovering a nourishing life-style there are no "shoulds" about how or with whom we relate. Multiple relationships, two-people intimacy or a lack of interest in intimate relating of any kind are a matter of each individual's needs and choices.

Rather than passively conforming to a traditional life-style or to a currently popular social trend, the nourishing person experiments to discover what fits *him* or *her* best.

In many ways an Intimacy of Two clearly limits our contact with and relating to other people. Any relationship to which we give our time and energy *always* means giving up some possibilities for other, different relationships *and* styles of relating.

Self-poisoning patterns emerge when we believe that, without paying a price, we can indulge ourselves in spontaneous, uninhibited gratification of our needs to relate to as many people as we wish in whatever ways we choose, without paying a price for it.

Multiple relationships by their very nature are more transient and superficial than two-person relationships. Their changing composition is usually considered as an advantage by those who are not interested in involving them-

selves in a commitment toward an enduring one-to-one relationship.

The person who wants to sustain an Intimacy of Two
and at the same time seeks similar intimacy with others
diminishes the gratification that either way of relating can
bring.

**Any existing intimate relationship is threatened by
the emerging possibility of a newly developing intimate relationship.**

There is no way to avoid this reality since we cannot
relate to two other people and give them our full attention
at the same time. When we imagine that we are fully relating to more than one person simultaneously, we are
actually shifting the focus of our attention, however rapidly,
from one person to another.

**A human being can give his full attention to only
one activity at a time, one experience at a time or
one person at a time.**

Multiple relating means splitting our attention and
diluting the meaningfulness of each separate relationship.
One-to-one relating unavoidably limits our ability to relate

to others even though there are obviously many people each of us might find interesting and attractive. There is no way we can have our cake and eat it too.

The ability of a man or woman to enjoy his or her relationships with any number of other people with *equal* intensity and gratification is simply a manifestation of the lack of an existing Intimacy of Two.

Multiple relating and two-people relating are antagonistic to each other. To the degree that we choose one, we hamper our ability to experience the other.

The person who is deeply involved in an Intimacy of Two *is* limited in his availability to other people. Conversely, the person who feels intimately involved with any number of other people *is* less available for an Intimacy of Two.

For years Lana had avoided and feared intimacy. An attractive woman, in her middle twenties, she had always felt free to enjoy herself sexually. When she was attracted to someone, she would take the initiative and make her wishes clear. These experiences were usually sexually satisfying; yet she preferred not to see the same person too often or for too long a period of time. When the other person wanted to continue the relationship, her reluctance would intensify.

Lana enjoyed sex more when there was a lack of intimacy in the relationship. When the relationship began to be more than sexual, she became increasingly anxious and her sexual responsiveness would diminish. By constantly meeting new people, she was able to avoid her fear of an intimate relationship. She did not want any commitment and, at least for the present, preferred multiple relationships, and these only on a superficial level.

Those who are interested in an Intimacy of Two may, of course, feel sexually attracted to other people. N people decide by their actions which is more important and more meaningful; the need for an enduring intimate relationship or the need for variety in one's sex life. Both are mutually antagonistic. While multiple relationships per se do not doom an Intimacy of Two, they are liable to be destructive and, in particular, to undermine the growth and durability of the relationship.

Sexual freedom is advocated by some as a means of avoiding the resentment that a person may feel if he decides to restrict his relating to others sexually. This is another unavoidable frustration. When we are sexually active with others, this *will* affect the other person with whom we are intimately involved even when there is mutual consent.

As the Intimacy of Two deepens, our willingness to share the other sexually becomes increasingly unlikely.

Sexual exclusiveness and an unwillingness to share one's mate (call it selfishness if you will) are readily observable in many higher species of animal life as well as in man. There are strong physiological and biological data to support the naturalness of this kind of unsharing, possessive love, which is one of the intrinsic qualities of an Intimacy of Two.

Many people poison their intimate relating by refusing to accept the consequences of their actions.

All of us resent giving up any of our freedom. On one level none of us ever gives up wanting everything we want exactly when we want it. We simply come to recognize that these impulses, while natural, realistically have consequences we are unwilling to risk. When a person makes a choice of sharing intimate aspects of himself with a third person instead of his Intimate Other, he takes some risk of jeopardizing his one-to-one relationship.

In an Intimacy of Two the nourishing person is aware when his actions or responsiveness to his own needs may be toxic to his Intimate Other and detrimental to their relationship.

In a nourishing Intimacy of Two the restrictions each person accepts on his separate freedom are not in any way a surrendering of the separate identities for the sake of the relationship. Both individuals understand that at times their feelings of intimacy and love may recede into the background of their needs for various reasons.

In an Intimacy of Two the relationship is not by any means always in the center of each person's needs.

Part of an intimate relationship of two *is* their ability and willingness of the two to allow themselves and the other to withdraw, to be preoccupied elsewhere and to be less involved in the relationship at various times. This is essential in order to avoid poisoning the relationship by excessive togetherness, which endangers the ability of each person to experience his or her separate self and maintain his or her inner intimacy.

When one person in an Intimacy of Two is polygamous, the other also has this option—even when it may not be his or her preference. The person who is not so interested in multiple intimacies as his partner, however, may feel a void in his own emotional fulfillment, a void that he cannot satisfy by himself or in other intimate relationships.

It takes two to nourish an intimate relationship. It takes only one to poison it.

The likelihood, then, of an enduring Intimacy of Two is diminished. The feeling of mutual commitment necessary for a sustained intimacy is further lessened by the continuous availability of numerous other people with whom one or both are intimate.

Those who advocate multiple relationships, open marriage, communal living or "free love" usually emphasize the rich potentials of not being "hemmed in" by one other person.

People who insist on doing their own thing are invariably toxic in their relating to others.

The nourishing person is aware that he is the most important person in the world to himself; he is also aware that his behavior does not take place in a vacuum and that being his own person does not mean ignoring the effect of his actions on his Intimate Other. His actions *will* have consequences, and it is his responsibility to be aware when his relating to others may have detrimental effects on his one-to-one intimacy.

Rick and Lucy enjoyed a deep, stable relationship—an Intimacy of Two. They had been living together for three years while each pursued graduate studies in separate disciplines. They were interested in a future together, and both were committed to sexual fidelity. Their available time together was, of necessity, markedly limited.

Rick was also attracted to Joyce, a graduate student in his department. They decided they could enjoy each other sexually and no one would be hurt. Almost immediately after Rick began his affair with Joyce, Lucy sensed a change. Although he continued to make love as frequently as in the past, Lucy felt his passion weaken. Whenever she commented on this, Rick would reply that he was under pressure at school.

As Rick's affair continued, Lucy became panicked that they were drifting apart. Rick was seeing Joyce more and more frequently. He was fully aware that his interest was largely sexual, that he still preferred Lucy's company and felt more relaxed with her.

His intent was to not deprive Lucy of her sexual needs and at the same time allow himself the passion of his affair. Yet Rick had his secret, and the openness and intimacy between him and Lucy began to diminish. When she told him she felt they were losing each other, his response was little more than a superficial reassurance.

Months passed, and although Lucy still did not know that Rick was having an affair, she continued to feel Rick's diminishing availability and caring, until eventually she realized that she no longer felt committed to him and told him so.

Rick was shattered. He expressed his love for Lucy, confessed his affair and promised to end it. Initially, Lucy was furious at Rick's betrayal. She then reluctantly agreed that they would try to renew their relationship. But their mutual effort lasted only a few weeks. Both realized that they could not re-establish the intimacy they had known—and lost. In spite of the love she still felt for Rick, Lucy ended their relationship convinced that her trust in him had been irreparably destroyed, and that, try as she might, she could not let herself become open and vulnerable to him again.

Rick had had no intention of jeopardizing his intimacy with Lucy. He had not wanted to leave Lucy because of his sexual attraction to Joyce. He had been playing a version of the "I can have my cake and eat it too" game. He had been unaware of what the consequences of his affair would be if Lucy found out. After their final breakup Rick went into a deep depression lasting for several months. He repeatedly tried to renew his relationship with Lucy but to no avail. He rebuked himself for his stupidity and mourned the loss of his relationship with Lucy. These feelings, although sincere, were nothing more than an exercise in futility. What was done was done.

In their quest for a growing and enduring intimacy most couples are aware that sexuality can be a potential source of disruption to their overall intimacy. It is essential to seek the resolution to any such conflicts within the framework of their overall life-style and mutual interaction.

SEXUAL FIDELITY

MARY (*to her best friend*): I'm really bothered—John is such a good husband. He's wonderful with the kids, and I love him in many ways. But I'm bored with our sex life. He's so mechanical I can predict just what he will do when we make love and almost precisely when he'll do it. I've talked to him about it, but he only gets irritated and asks what I expect after eight years of marriage. Now something else has happened. Remember when I met Hank at your party a few months ago? Well, we've met for lunch a few times. He wants to have an affair with me. He loves his wife but feels we can be adult about it, enjoy each other, and nobody will get hurt.

JOHN (*to his best friend, Bill*): I need to talk. Suzy [John's secretary] and I have had to work late several times, and we've been flirting with each other. She really turns me on. You know how much I love Mary [John's wife] but I can feel the pressure building.

BILL: Why not just be discreet about it and have a quiet affair? What's the harm if you're careful so Mary doesn't find out? Nobody will get hurt.

Choosing a one-to-one intimacy means accepting responsibility for whatever resentment and frustration may occur when we limit our freedom and availability for relationships with others.

Those who choose multiple sexual intimacy risk jeopardizing their Intimacy of Two. The power of emotions is often not fully appreciated. A sexual relationship is frequently the gateway to a deeper, broader emotional involvement whether or not this is intended. The agreement between two people to have an affair and "keep it light so no one will be hurt" is the kind of good intention which totally ignores the power of human emotions.

PART THREE

ANTIDOTES

8

AWARENESS, COMMUNICATION
AND CONFRONTATION

Most antidotes to toxic relating are simple, *and* they
are not easy.

Despite the fantastic variety of toxic games with which
people poison their intimacy, our ability to understand
these complex patterns is greatly enhanced when we become
aware that only a limited number of attitudes and kinds of
behavior characterize toxic interaction. Just being aware of
these will suggest the approaches each of us can experiment with in order to discover our own most effective antidotes. When we are willing to do our own trial-and-error
experimenting, we can discover which antidotes best suit

us personally, i.e., which are most effective and harmonious with the uniqueness of our own self.

Awareness, communication and confrontation are the three phases of the basic process in all effective antidotes. The critical issue in seeking creative resolutions to toxic patterns rests on our interest and willingness to commit ourselves to enhancing the development of all three phases of the antidote process first within our separate selves *and* secondly sharing these with our Intimate Other.

Awareness as an Antidote

Once we see what we do to poison our Intimate Other and how we allow our Intimate Other to poison us, the way is open to new possibilities for more nourishing relating.

Awareness of *what* we do to poison our intimacy and *how* we do this is the royal road to the discovery of the antidotes to toxic patterns in our intimate relationships.

Awareness is the first ingredient for change. To seek antidotes to the toxic aspects of our intimacy, we must be aware of our frustrations in important areas of our relating with our Intimate Other. This seems simple enough; yet a major way in which we create toxic patterns in the first place is by *avoiding the obvious.* Our excuses for this are usually some kind of rationalization, judgmentalness or fear of making things worse. ("If I ignore the toxic patterns in our relationship, maybe somehow they will go away by themselves.") Awareness of painful feelings such as anxiety, fear or resentment toward our Intimate Other is a hallmark of toxic interaction. Acknowledging (rather than ignoring) these symptoms is the beginning of the discovering of the antidotes.

> SANDRA: I'm tired of trying to laugh off your jealousy and my explaining myself every time I'm half an hour late.
> LOU: I'm sorry I upset you. It's only because I love you so much.
> SANDRA: I believe you, and *that* kind of love is making me resentful. I'm aware that I'm turning off toward you. I hoped that you would gradually feel more secure and trusting, but the more I try to reassure you, the more re-assurance you seem to demand.
> LOU: I do trust you, but I see how men look at you. I don't trust them.
> SANDRA: I can't do anything about that. I feel scared telling you this, but I know how resentful I feel when you inter-rogate me. I'm going to stop accounting to you about my free time.

In this dialogue Sandra finally allows herself to be fully aware of her resentments, which she had felt all along and tried to avoid.

Full Awareness Usually Impels Action

She begins to seek a solution (antidote) by expressing her feelings openly and fully to Lou and taking a stand. Whether her initial experiment (not accounting to Lou for her time) turns out to be an effective antidote is secondary to her now being willing to face her own resentments and beginning the process of experimentation to counteract this toxic aspect of their relationship.

Communication as an Antidote: What and How in the Here And Now

Our anxieties and fears tend to intensify as we venture into unknown territory, experimenting with new attitudes and behavior patterns. Awareness is only half the battle. We must also be willing to initiate new ways of being and relating if any real change is to occur.

Communicating our dissatisfaction to our Intimate Other brings our fears and anxieties into fuller awareness. It is part of the risk-taking process which is unavoidable. The open expression of our dissatisfactions with our Intimate Other easily raises the fear that the relationship itself may be in jeopardy. Yet without it our Intimate Other is left only with fantasies about what is happening to their relationship. The possibilities of Lou's cooperation in resolving the toxic pattern is also eliminated. In the above dialogue Sandra tells Lou *what* he is doing that is toxic (his jealousy) and *how* it is poisoning their Intimacy (his interrogating her). In communicating this to Lou she shares her awareness of this toxic pattern and, in so doing, opens the possibility that he himself may explore with her what he might do to resolve the conflict. At the same time, and this is most basic, Sandra initiates her own, independent efforts at seeking an antidote.

> The most common way in which we poison our intimacy with another is to seek our antidotes and well-being *primarily* through relationships with others *rather than* from within ourselves. This reversal of the cart and the horse has endless toxic implications.

A growing awareness and understanding of the other person and how he or she relates to us can lead to *our* discovering new ways of relating to our Intimate Other in a more-nourishing, less-toxic manner. The following technique is a method of "putting one's self in the other person's shoes" by role-playing at being him.*

Being Your Intimate Other

Find a room where you can be alone. Arrange two chairs face to face. Now, sitting in one chair, imagine that your Intimate Other is sitting across from you, and start talking as if he or she were actually sitting there. Say whatever you feel like saying. To feel the emotional impact of this technique, it is essential that you talk out loud as if your Intimate Other were really there. When you run out of things to say, change seats and role-play being your Intimate Other replying to you. Don't be a mimic; rather, be your Intimate Other any way that *you* feel like. Continue your dialogue, changing seats back and forth whenever you want

---

* This is a widely used method in Gestalt therapy through which a person enhances his awareness and discovers new possibilities for experimentation and creative resolutions to his conflicts.

to as you create your script moment by moment. Most people feel silly, embarrassed or anxious when they start talking aloud to themselves. These feelings usually diminish rapidly. This role-playing technique is surprisingly effective in deepening insight into a relationship. It often suggests how we can experiment by exploring new and different ways of relating that may be more gratifying. This technique helps us project ourselves into the other person. In any relationship, how *we* experience the other *is* the most significant aspect of the Intimate Relationship.

There is no such thing as objectively seeing the other "as he or she really is." Since we can see the world and others only through our own eyes, projection is inevitable and universal.

The following dialogue took place during an initial psychological consultation. Donna made the appointment because of the disruption of her relationship with her husband, Ron. He had refused to come with her. Donna talked about her various grievances and the conflicts that she and her husband seemed unable to resolve.

The therapist asked her to imagine that Don was sitting in an empty chair a few feet in front of her and to role-play as if she were an actress, writing her own script and saying whatever she wanted to her husband. Donna felt embarrassed, but she was willing to try the experiment. There was a moment's pause. She stared at the empty chair.

DONNA (*turning to her therapist*): I don't know what to say to him.

THERAPIST: Say that to Ron as if he were sitting there.

DONNA (*turning to face the empty chair*): Ron, I don't know what to say to you. . . . It's true I find it very hard to talk to you. You always have some logical answer—some simply logical answer to whatever I am concerned about. I wish we could just talk together like we used to. (*Donna is silent and seems at a loss as to how to continue.*)

THERAPIST: Now change seats and be Ron and reply to what you just said to him.

(*Donna smiles, changes seats and looks toward the chair she just left.*)

DONNA (*playing her husband*): You just create problems. You make mountains out of molehills. We don't really have any conflicts. Our marriage is better than any of our friends'—look at how many people we know who are divorced. (*Donna spontaneously changes seats and is now herself again, talking to her husband in the empty chair.*) See, that's what I mean! You cut off the discussion with one sweeping statement. You don't leave me any room to say what's bothering me. You put me down, and you make me feel silly or childish when I'm bothered by something. What kind of relationship is that?

(*Therapist gestures to Donna to change seats again and play the part of her husband.*)

DONNA (*being her husband*): I think we both have it pretty good. I'm tired of your complaining. I'm not going to change. I like things the way they are. (*Donna changes seats and again is herself responding to her husband in the empty chair.*) You're impossible! Talking to you is like talking to a stone wall.

Following this role-playing dialogue, Donna became more acutely aware of how she was frustrating herself by her repeatedly futile attempts to communicate with her husband. She decided to continue therapy in order to become more aware of herself and her own role and in the hope of discovering new ways of dealing with her conflicts on her own as well as experimenting with new approaches to relating to her husband.

A short time later Donna began to get herself unstuck by putting into action her new awareness. First she stopped frustrating herself by letting go of her "sales campaign"—trying to get Ron to listen to her. She began to focus more on herself, on what she needed to express and wanted to communicate to her husband. She stayed centered on her self and *her* need to communicate. She began to accept (recognize) that Ron really didn't listen to her. She no longer frustrated herself waiting for a positive response that never came. Instead she stated *her* reaction to his comments for *her own benefit* and allowed him to respond in whatever way he chose—including not to respond.

On one occasion she actually said, "Talking to you is like talking to a wall," just as she had done when she was role playing, and left the room. This was what she was experiencing, and this is what she needed to say for *herself*. As she became increasingly aware of the futility of having a real dialogue with her husband, she began to turn her energies elsewhere, renewing friendships and activities she had given up when she and Ron married. She felt a great sadness and longing for Ron and also now realized that:

It takes two people to communicate. One person cannot create real contact and communication when the other is uninterested or unwilling.

Ron cared deeply for Donna, and it was only after some months of experiencing her withdrawal from him that he began to pay serious attention (really listen) to what she had been telling him. Donna had never played sex-withholding games, and during these months the frequency of their sexual contact remained the same. It continued to be one area in which she could feel a sense of intimacy and sharing with Ron. She was aware, however, of a lessening of her responsiveness. She understood this and felt saddened by it too. She chose not to share it with Ron. Much to her surprise, he expressed to her his own awareness of this and for the first time began to "hear" what Donna had been telling him (verbally) for so long. He finally began to listen, and the possibility of real communication emerged.

Confrontation as an Antidote

Confrontation, the third phase of the basic antidote process, represents the critical *points of action* and is a culmination of the prior development of our awareness and communication. Despite our fears and anxieties the need for confrontation with ourselves and our Intimate Other emerges spontaneously when we are unwilling to continue a pattern of toxic interaction.

Confrontation means taking a definite stand against
the continuation of a toxic pattern and is always a
risk-taking procedure since it involves some threat
to the continuation of the relationship.

Confrontation begins with the self. Step one means we
focus our own awareness of our frustration about some
aspect of our relationship with our Intimate Other. We
bring this awareness into the *center* of our attention. An in-
ternal communication (dialogue with ourselves) usually
follows. This inner awareness—communication—confrontation process is how we mobilize our energies until we are
ready to risk the taking of action to seek remedy.

Antidotes always involve action whether on our own
or with the cooperation of our Intimate Other.

Such actions often mean terminating our own contribu-
tion to the perpetuation of a toxic pattern of relating. When
we confront ourselves effectively with our part in the toxic
process—however passive our role may be—the major road-
block to finding an antidote (if one is possible, and this is
not always true) has been removed.

Other self-confrontations include taking an active stand
to initiate and experiment with new responses toward the

toxic patterns of relating which we experience from our Intimate Other. In the case of Lou's jealousy, Sandra confronted both herself (first) and Lou with a new way of reacting to his jealousy by refusing to continue her previous pattern of submitting to his interrogations about her activities.

Confrontation, then, involves *activating* a new attitude and way of relating *and* giving up (letting go of) an existing pattern that has been ineffective and contributes to allowing the toxic pattern to continue.

An Intimacy of Two grows stronger when we confront our Intimate Other with what we experience as toxic and he or she responds cooperatively.

Antidotes to toxic relating are most effective when each person takes responsibility for his part in the toxic interaction *and* both are interested in exploring all aspects of the problem together.

Owning One's Power

It is nourishing to appreciate and enjoy those qualities in an Intimate Other that enhance the meaningfulness of our relationship. It is toxic when, in appreciating the other, we fail to recognize that our responsiveness is also a reflection of *our own* potential coming into bloom in a nourishing relationship. We then attribute our well-being to the other person instead of recognizing that an intimate relationship brings forth new potentials from within us.

> The stronger our own sense of identity, the deeper our intimacy with ourselves, the greater our potential for an enduring, growing intimate relationship with another.

Without awareness of this reality we are liable to place burdens and demands on our Intimate Other, whom we see as our main source of strength. This sets the stage for the possessiveness, jealousy and demands that are destructive to the relationship.

One of the best ways to turn into fact the fear that the other person will leave us is to keep telling him or her how afraid we are of being rejected. In projecting our own fear, we dump the burden on the other. Trying to get our Intimate Other to take responsibility for our fears and anxieties is manipulative and therefore toxic. What is even more toxic is that in so doing we relinquish our power and make ourselves helpless.

> Without self-trust, an essential ingredient of the intimate self, those things we fear most are the very things we are liable to bring on ourselves.

There Ain't No Hiding Place Down There

CONNIE: It's a sickness of the soul. That's how I feel . . . kind of terrible. . . . It shouldn't be so difficult. I don't understand why I can't let go of him. Really I don't. I'm trying so hard. It's too painful and frightening. I can't stand it.

THERAPIST: Could you verbalize your pain and your fright? Face it for a little while?

CONNIE: My pain is that . . . I can't believe that I could live with someone for a year and a half and feel the way we felt . . . and have him turn around and end it the way he did . . . without any explanation, without any feeling, without any kindness . . . like I'm not even a person. I'll never, ever get over that. My pain is that I was so humiliated and degraded.

THERAPIST: Say this to Bob. Put him there (*in an empty chair*) and tell him how outraged you are.

CONNIE (*role-playing by talking to the empty chair as if Bob were sitting in it*): It's not a matter of your not loving me any more—there's no painless way to tell somebody that. But it is the way you handled it. You put me in a position where I had to say to you, "You don't love me any more, do you?" And you said, "No." That was so shitty! If you had just sat down and talked to me, if you had just sat down and told me how you felt. . . . It's so ugly now, so ugly. I'm so afraid. If I don't stop you, I'll just suffer one more humiliation after another, one more rejection after another, and I can't stand any more. . . . I can't. I don't like it. I don't like your behavior. . . . (*Turning toward the therapist*) He was very different. That's another thing. In the beginning he was . . .

THERAPIST: Tell him how he changed.

CONNIE (*continuing to role-play as if Bob were present*): It was roses and "I love you" cards. You acted as if I was a queen. And then all of a sudden you see I'm a real person. I wasn't allowed to make any mistakes, have any fears, be insecure, have any needs. You gave me so much, and then you took it all away. Just one day you looked at me so coldly, and now I feel it was all a lie! I can't believe you ever really loved me, now . . . and that's what frightens me . . . that I was with you a whole year and a half and you never really cared. . . . Was it all a show? I can't believe that. But I can't believe that you can love someone so much and now this.

THERAPIST: You sound like you believed everything from the very beginning and just followed along like a naïve little lamb.

CONNIE: I didn't have any idea what was happening. All I know is that one day he started to act a little funny— that's all I knew. Until one day I did say to him—it was always this way, I always had to be the one to ask—I said, "What's wrong—is there something wrong?" I asked him, and he said he wanted to date other women. And I said, "Fine, you can date other women, but you can't date me too." I told him what I needed and what I could handle, and I could not handle that kind of situation.

THERAPIST: What are you avoiding paying attention to?

CONNIE: I know what it is. I didn't say, "I don't feel like you love me." That's what I didn't say, and that's what I was feeling. I was feeling not very loved, and I was afraid to say that I was feeling that way. Instead, I continued to put the whole thing in his hands—I put myself in his hands. I really felt loved. I felt very accepted and wanted. I don't know that I felt loved right from the beginning, but practically. . . . But I did worry all the time.

THERAPIST: What did you do with your worry?

CONNIE: I did what I thought was the right thing to do— which was to go back into therapy and talk about it.

THERAPIST: That's not taking responsibility for yourself. You still weren't confronting Bob with how you're experiencing him.

CONNIE: Yes . . . I knew what I could have done. I put myself in a very bad position in that relationship, and I did it not just once but twice. The second time I had a choice of saying to Bob, when he came back and said, "I love you, you're the only one in the world for me, and I don't want anybody else." I could have recognized right then that it was a lie . . . his way of keeping me in the picture. Regardless of how he felt. I feel now that what I wish I had done was say, "That is all very well and good, and that's nice, but I think we should date. . . . I think I should get my own house, you have your house, and we'll see how things work out. We can still see each other." I didn't protect myself in this relationship. I gave him all my power.

Connie learned from the pain of her experience that her attempts to avoid her own awareness that all was not well in her relationship with Bob only postponed her distress and made the inevitable confrontation far more painful than it might have been.

Playing ostrich is a way of rendering ourselves impotent while the reality of any relationship eventually emerges sooner or later.

9

TOXIC FREEDOM (YOU ONLY LIVE ONCE SO TAKE ALL YOU CAN GET) AND ITS ANTIDOTE

There was an old woman who lived in a shoe,
She had so many children she didn't know what to do.
So she did the best she could for all of them,
And couldn't help spreading herself very thin.

An Intimacy of Two does not mean that we can be all things to the other or that we don't need other meaningful relationships. However, the "I want to have my cake and eat it too" life-style implies that an Intimacy of Four or Eight or Fifty is just as natural and healthy, or even more so, in meeting our emotional needs as an Intimacy of Two. The hook on which people catch themselves is the popular myth that emotionally secure, emotionally mature people do not need a single Intimate Other or want an exclusive specialness with an other.

This attitude is a reflection of the great American myth that we cannot have too much freedom; that the freer we are, the better off we are and the happier we will be.

In our intimate relationships, when we declare ourselves free of restrictions and commitments, we diminish or even eliminate the value of any particular other person.

In intimate relating, freedom of choice becomes toxic when we feel that any one person in our lives is easily replaceable by another or when such transitions occur without significant pain or feeling of loss.

Many people become trapped in their own toxic games by their chronic anti-Victorian rebellion against any restrictions or inhibitions.

While this attitude is most prevalent in sexuality, it occurs—albeit less dramatically—in other aspects of their relationships.

No one ever really gives up wanting exactly what he

wants exactly when he wants it. We simply learn that fully expressing our impulses would have consequences that would be disastrous, that having things our own way can become an indiscriminate permissiveness, a runaway toxic self indulgence. In this condition, self-control, discipline and plain, old-fashioned will power are considered "bad." Those who have been sold the fantasy that inhibition is toxic per se do not develop the ability to sustain themselves in the face of frustration or adversity. Instead they fly into tantrums, give up easily or sulk helplessly when they don't get what they want. ("What did I do to deserve such bad luck?")

In an Intimacy of Two, we poison the relationship when we expect that each person can do his own thing and there will be no important conflicts to interfere with our intimacy.

In an Intimacy of Two, giving up some of our freedom for the sake of maintaining the relationship is absolutely unavoidable.

JOHN: How about a movie tonight?

MARY: O.K.

JOHN: I'd like to see movie A.

MARY: I want to see movie B.

JOHN: I prefer movie A, and since I don't want to stifle myself, I'm going to movie A alone.

MARY: Fine, I feel the same way. I'm going to movie B. I'll see you later.

In this example, there is no effort to seek a compromise. Such excessive permissiveness toward our own selves erodes intimacy by unnecessarily limiting sharing and contact.

In an Intimacy of Two any antidote to conflict requires that each be willing to give up some freedom in order to reach a compromise with the other.

Antidotes are rarely effective when they reflect extreme attitudes or dogmatic decisions. John's and Mary's refusal even to negotiate a compromise ("I'll go with you this time if you go with me next time") is likely to reflect their individual insecurities. When we lack inner intimacy, we feel more threatened by the give-and-take necessary in an Intimacy of Two. Since all of us have insecurities, antidotes to toxic relating become easier to achieve when each person accepts his own and his Intimate Other's anxieties and other hangups without judging either or in any way implying that either "should change."

It is *not* toxic to feel insecure, anxious or "neurotic." It is *how* we relate to ourselves and our Intimate Other about such feelings that can produce toxic interaction.

The antidote involves giving up the toxic patterns of judgmentalness toward our self or our Intimate Other or playing comparison games. ("You're more neurotic than I am.")

The realization that we don't *have* to change or be different can free us from so much toxic pressure ("I/you better change or else!") that such awareness in itself is a powerful antidote.

When we accept this attitude, we actually regain a great deal of our own power and energy which otherwise remains lost in the futile process of endlessly pressuring (trying to force) ourselves to change.

10

THE POISON OF PERMISSIVENESS . . .
AND ITS ANTIDOTE

Toxic permissiveness of the "I do my thing, you do your thing" brand is an extension of the general permissive attitude of our culture. It is exemplified in "open marriage," which implies that two people can continue an enduring intimate relationship and neither need give up pursuing his personal quest for total satisfaction of his own self-centered needs.

The appeal of "open marriage" is another example of the permissiveness myth that encourages us to think that we can be omnipotent. It says, "You can be your own person to the fullest extent of your capabilities and so can your partner. At the same time, the two of you can share an intimate life-style together that will grow in stability and durability." This is a myth, and it has no relation to the reality of an Intimacy of Two.

Frustration Is Evil

HUSBAND: Damn it! The mechanic says we need a couple of hundred dollars' work on the car—and just as we made the last payment!

WIFE: There's always something. I'm getting used to expecting unexpected expenses.

HUSBAND: It's not fair. I think they make cars so they break down just about the time you have them paid off, so you have to buy a new one.

WIFE: We don't have to buy a new one. We can have this one fixed and save a lot of money.

HUSBAND: Then we still have a used car, and something else will go wrong. Let's trade it in on a new one.

WIFE: Remember when we figured out that if we gave up buying our cars on a payment plan we would actually get every fifth car free just by saving the interest and loan costs?

HUSBAND: I know that's true, but I just can't stand the aggravation of having to get that damn car fixed every time something goes wrong. Let's go get a new one now. You can pick the color.

WIFE: Well—all right. I don't want you to get angry, and I don't want to fight with you.

This example typifies the kind of excessive permissiveness and self-indulgence that are toxic both to the individual and to his intimate relating to others. The husband's comments reveal his insistence on having his way, and having it right now (frustration intolerance). This attitude is a manifestation of the toxic myth that pain is somehow bad. He expects that he should not have to tolerate the pain (frustration, impatience) of putting up with a car that is less reliable than a new one, despite the real strain that giving in to his impulses will have on the family budget.

In the dialogue both husband and wife are generating a toxic process in their relationship. (Couples fight over money more than any other issue.) Although the husband is the principal instigator because of his unrealistic self-indulgent attitude, the wife is contributing to the inevitable stress of future financial strain by giving in and rationalizing her refusal to continue to take her stand. It is *not* her responsibility to stop her husband from giving in to his lack of frustration tolerance. However, she could use her own awareness-communication-confrontation process to sustain her own conviction as her best antidote to her husband's toxic self-permissiveness. In this way she hands him the full responsibility for the consequences of his impulsiveness. It is hoped that the husband will learn that he frustrates himself much more by his self-indulgence—but this will be a matter of whether (and when) *he* chooses to confront himself with his own awareness.

Our willingness to tolerate legitimate pain and frustration is an essential attitude in seeking antidotes to toxic patterns of all kinds.

In an Intimacy of Two both people feel that whatever relating with others they agree to forgo is *more* than compensated for by the joy, excitement and growth they experience together and that the loss of their intimacy would leave each with far greater feelings of deprivation.

Total freedom in a relationship is the hallmark of the impulse-ridden person who rejects the fact that reality means continual unavoidable choices.

11

VIOLATIONS OF PSYCHIC SPACE . . .
AND THEIR ANTIDOTES

HOWARD (*who has been feeling very loving all evening*):
Come on, honey, let's go to bed.

VALERY: You go ahead. I'll be in later.

HOWARD: It's been such a lovely evening I thought you
would want to . . .

VALERY (*cutting him off*): Now don't get mad. It has been
a lovely evening and . . . I don't feel like making love
tonight.

HOWARD: I'm not mad. . . . I do feel rejected . . .

VALERY (*cutting him off again*): That's what I mean.
Whenever I don't want to make love, you act so hurt
and make me feel guilty.

HOWARD: *That's* what makes me mad. I want to make love
and you don't. O.K. When you don't want to make love,
I get turned off anyway. But you want me to act happy
and smile about it, and I don't feel that way. Why can't

you allow me to feel hurt or sulk or whatever I feel like doing when I feel rejected?

VALERY: You make me feel guilty. And I don't want you to make me feel guilty.

HOWARD: There's no need for you to feel guilty. That makes me angry.

The toxic interaction begins when *each* is not willing to accept the other's reaction. Howard feels rejected and Valery feels guilty about rejecting him.

In an Intimacy of Two, each at times feels angry, detached or uninterested and accepts the other's right to whatever reaction he or she feels.

Toxic interaction arises when we will not allow each other separate, different reactions to a disagreement. When we tell each other not to get angry or feel guilty, we are being judgmental and critical. What we are saying is, "Why don't you react the way *I* would like you to? I don't want to accept your right to react in whatever way *you* choose."

Ideally, in an intimate relationship there are no limits to our acceptance (recognition) of the reality of what's going on within the other person (while not necessarily liking it).

HOWARD (*grinning*): O.K. Tell you what I'm going to do. You allow me to feel hurt, and I'll allow you to feel guilty.

VALERY: You got a deal! (*Both laugh and hold each other.*)

The most prevalent toxic pattern that poisons intimacy is the refusal to allow ourselves and our intimate other to be exactly where we are emotionally (psychic space) without feeling we are wrong or shouldn't feel as we do.

This toxic attitude usually imposes an expectation that in an intimate relationship we are entitled to certain rights and privileges that are to be cheerfully provided by the other.

In an Intimacy of Two the fewer the expectations of each about the fulfillments and gratifications that will be forthcoming from the other, the greater the likelihood that the relationship is a nourishing one. Conversely, the more the two look to their intimate involvement as a solution to their inner frustrations and dissatisfactions, the greater the likelihood that toxic patterns will develop.

T people usually reject the reality that many, if not most, of their frustrations are only indirectly, if at all, a legitimate part of their relationship.

Relating intimately means using our power of self-expression and self-assertion to do the best we can to get what we need. In the nourishing use of our aggressive power, we are willing to take a stand and say what we want.

When the other person does not choose to respond to us as we would like, the nourishing person does not try to coerce him into being more responsive. Rather, he respects the other's integrity by allowing him the same freedom of reaction and self-expression which he seeks for himself. To avoid being toxic toward the other, he seeks the resolution of his needs by turning his attention elsewhere. He does not do this in anger or vengeance against the Intimate Other. Rather, he recognizes that the other's lack of responsiveness is simply a statement of their separateness. This manifestation of mutual respect for each other's integrity is expressed in a willingness to allow the self and the Intimate Other whatever space (mood) each is in.

Toxic conflict that is so destructive to an intimate relationship is in marked contrast to this. It takes the form of power struggles, manipulation, persuasion and other attempts to coerce the Intimate Other out of his or her position into at least passive compliance.

12

TOXIC ATTITUDES TOWARD INSECURITY . . . AND THEIR ANTIDOTE

PATTY: I'm jealous when I see you talking to other women. I'm afraid I'm not enough for you.

GEORGE: I wish you didn't have these hangups. You're totally unreasonable to feel that way. You ought to get some help with these things and learn to grow up!

The toxic myth that a mature person does not have any "unreasonable" fears or anxieties can poison an Intimacy of Two by implying that the other should outgrow them. Although it may be very gratifying when both people in an intimate relationship feel secure and trusting, often this is not the case.

> To denounce the insecurities of our Intimate Other
> or insist that they should not affect the relationship
> is toxic.

This does not mean that we are to assume responsibility
for the insecurities of the other but rather that we could
recognize that the other's fears and anxieties *do* exist and
avoid condemning him or expecting that he or she will (or
should) overcome them.

IT TAKES TWO TO HAVE A CONVERSATION

KATHY: I'm angry at you for leaving me alone at the party
last night. You knew I didn't know anyone and . . .

TIM: I saw you talking to some people, and I didn't know
you were alone.

KATHY: I was talking to someone for a while but . . .

TIM: I'm sorry I didn't pay more attention. I really didn't
know you were alone.

KATHY: You just don't see me as a person. You . . .

TIM: Now, that's unfair to make that generalization. I know
I was wrong last night, and I apologize. I will try to be
more aware next time.

KATHY: I know you mean well, but . . .

TIM: Kathy, let's not make a major issue out of this. Let's
forget it and enjoy ourselves now.

KATHY (*becoming increasingly angry*): I'm not finished dis-
cussing this yet. I have more to say . . .

TIM: All right. What do you want from me? What's it
going to take for me to square things with you?

Kathy is self-poisoning when she persistently tries to express herself when Tim wants only to end the argument. Kathy poisons herself by not confronting *herself* with her dilemma. The antidote to this situation would be for her to ask herself, "What do *I* want to do when I am aware that Tim doesn't want to discuss my grievance with me?"

It is a toxic manipulation to try to change another despite one's good intentions. It is self-poisoning when we endlessly repeat ourselves, hoping that the other person will finally hear us and discontinue his poisonous behavior.

13

TOXIC CONFLICT IN INTIMACY . . . AND ITS ANTIDOTE

In any intimate relationship, there will be some continuing, even unresolvable conflicts. Each person may resent some attitudes or kinds of behavior that the other is not willing to give up. These conflicts are not necessarily warning signals that the relationship is in jeopardy. All human relationships are full of imperfections.

The illusion that our Intimate Other is the one who restricts our personal freedom remains a popular myth. This is reflected in toxic arguments, often chronic in nature, in which a couple continually fight over such issues as who cleans the house, who controls the money, what social functions they will attend and who shall be allowed sexual intercourse with whom.

In an Intimacy of Two the conflicts that arise concerning each person's individual frustrations are shared, and with an attitude that there is a common need to resolve the differences, a solution is sought.

In an Intimacy of Two, there is an absence of struggle by one person *against* the other. Most, if not all, arguments are warlike, and seeking to win over an Intimate Other is destructive no matter what the outcome.

When conflicts occur, it is important to recognize when our way of fighting and that of our Intimate Other differ. Withdrawal is just as reasonable (or unreasonable) a way of fighting as overwhelming one's opponent with words. Conflict is toxic when the two people have not found a mutually acceptable way to settle their grievances. The likelihood that such interaction will lead to a constructive resolution of their conflicts is remote.

Antidote: There is no set of rules by which two people should or should not fight with each other.

CHAPTER

14

THE BASIC ATTITUDE IN SEEKING ANTIDOTES: "THIS IS ME"

Being on intimate terms with ourselves means accepting our anxieties, our fears, our insecurities—rational or not— because they *are* part of us. We need not *like* these feelings and may want to become more secure or less fearful. Only when we relate to ourselves in this fashion do we have the potential to relate similarly to others.

To the degree that we love only part of ourselves and reject what we don't like, we remain fragmented and avoid the possibility of becoming a whole person.

An Intimacy of Two is often blocked in its depth by lack of love of those parts of the Intimate Other which are the same unpleasant, painful or unwanted parts we reject in ourselves.

Allowing the other person his insecurities, anxieties and fears is one of the milestones of a deeper Intimacy of Two.

This acceptance of the other person as a whole includes both what we like and appreciate and what we dislike or resent.

Nourishing: In my quest for intimacy do I want to continue my relationship with an Intimate Other as he or she is *now?*

or

Toxic: Am I living with the fantasy that our intimacy is so strong that it will motivate the other to change or give up what I find objectionable?

PART FOUR

FINDING, NOURISHING AND—SOMETIMES— SAYING GOODBYE TO YOUR INTIMATE OTHER

15

HOW TO FIND AN INTIMATE OTHER

Responsibility in intimate relating has nothing to do with duty or obligation. Rather, it is an attitude of *responsiveness* (respondability) to the Intimate Other.

Warning: Beware of seeking an intimate relationship with a person who repeatedly sends messages that "I'm just doing my thing" or in his relating responds to the other person's needs with "That's *your* thing."

The implication of these qualities is that the person is not really interested in responding to the needs of another.

Such people are usually sending a clear message (if we pay attention) that they are so involved with their self that in their relating they are essentially unavailable to anyone seeking an enduring one-to-one intimacy. The sooner we realize when we are trying to relate to an unresponsive person, the less of our lives we waste and the more we spare ourselves the pain of a toxic relationship.

Irreconcilable Differences

While solving conflicts through compromise is essential in any Intimacy of Two, a relationship becomes precarious when either person attempts to compromise needs and values that are central aspects of their separate identities. Such a compromise, although perhaps solving an immediate conflict, in the long run creates deep discord and resentment that arc likely to become increasingly difficult to reconcile.

Toxic Approach

JOHN: All my life I've planned to leave the city and live in a rural area. It's one of the main reasons why I became a veterinarian.

MARY: I've always enjoyed the advantages of living in a large city, but I think living in a rural area would be O.K. with me, especially since one of my dreams is to have a large family.

JOHN: I've always felt a large family would keep me tied down for too long a period of my life. However, if you're willing to go along with living in a rural area, I'll let you decide how many children you want to have.

Although compromise is usually nourishing in an Intimacy of Two, John and Mary are each giving up part of their basic needs and separate life-plans. Despite their good intentions they are setting the stage for possibly insurmountable resentments in the future.

When we forgo needs that are central to our life-plan and life-style, they tend to become sacrifices rather than compromises. In an Intimacy of Two, sacrificing is toxic.

In marked contrast to the previous dialogue is the way Bill and Jane share the excitement of discovering that their principal needs, life-style and life-plan are remarkably similar.

JANE: I'd like to have kids close together and while we're still young. Then we can be free to do what we want when our kids are grown.

BILL: I've always wanted a family, and I've always hoped that I will be able to do other things—just the two of us— as our children grow older. Even while they're still living at home, I'd like to travel as part of my life-style.

JANE: I've always wanted to explore other parts of the world even if I have to live on a meager budget to do it.

BILL: I feel doubly excited discovering that something that is so important to me is something that you want too.

16

IT TAKES TIME TO LOVE

Intimate relating is an alive, evolving process of interaction between two people. It does not just happen when the "right one" comes along. It does not develop quickly. Mutual discovery of who the other is and real acceptance of each other (including both nourishing and toxic qualities) take time. Instant intimacy is a popular distortion of real love-relationships. Intimacy grows through the nourishing experiences two people share. Each episode of this process contributes to the depth and richness of the relationship and the enhancement of the intimacy.

Sharing experiences with a particular other person which fail to elicit a *mutual* feeling of gratification may be an early warning suggesting that the likelihood of evolving a really intimate relationship is limited.

In relating to another, particularly when we have a strong longing and hope for an intimate relationship, we often poison ourselves by failing or refusing to see when mutual sharing lacks the feeling of growing intimacy with the other.

Al and Barbara had met when they were working on the campus newspaper. They were initially intrigued with their discovery that each planned to take the summer off to explore the United States and Mexico. They decided to make the journey together. It was a summer of rich experiences. But when they returned to school in the fall, they seemed unable to continue to relate to each other in the delightful way they had during the summer. They agreed that they could be no more than good friends.

Although they had enjoyed sharing many experiences, this sharing did not enhance their feelings of closeness and intimacy toward each other. They were simply absorbed by the venture in which they were both participating. When this ended they became more aware of how they actually felt about each other.

In seeking an intimate relationship it is important to be aware when the excitement, adventure and joys of the events occurring are the predominant force sustaining the relationship rather than the way each person experiences himself with the other.

An Intimacy of Two implies a feeling of connectedness and mutual contact. As the relationship grows, this contacting gives each an increasing familiarity with and understanding of the other. People who have established a truly intimate relationship require fewer and fewer words. Intimates can often sense where the other person is psychologically by nonverbal cues that other people would scarcely notice or, if they did, would not understand. For example, when one person is simply quiet, the Intimate Other may know that he is really angry. He may also know that his other needs his silence and will express himself openly when he is ready.

A couple in therapy may be asked to role-play each other. If a really intimate relationship has developed, they are able to do this with relative ease. Nonintimate couples are often perplexed when asked to play the role of the other. They may be unaware of various preferences of the other even after a relationship of many years. They may not know their other's favorite color, favorite composer or artist, favorite kind of books—all things they would have observed on numerous occasions if they were truly interested in their other.

Lack of interest is often expressed by lack of knowledge that would come from simple observation of what one's Intimate Other is like. The longer the relationship has existed, the more a lack of interest warns us that an intimate relationship is not likely to develop.

Nourishing: When I am rejected by my Intimate Other do I attempt to find a resolution within the framework of our continuing relationship?

or

Toxic: Do I rush to protect myself against further rejection by throwing up walls, acting indifferent or playing some kind of "Who needs you?" game?

Nourishing: When I am convinced that I have done all I can and that I am unable to find an acceptance basis for continuing a relationship, do I accept this reality and take responsibility for letting go and handling my own pain and sense of loss?

or

Toxic: Do I wallow in self-pity, play blaming games or try to convince myself that the other person was no good in the first place?

Fred was a successful architect in his early thirties who sought therapy because of periods of depression which often lasted for days at a time. Fred had always been shy; yet his father kept pushing him to be more sociable. "If you find a good woman to get behind you, you've got the ability to be a big success in life" was his father's attitude.

Fred wanted a woman who was simply herself, not overly aggressive or socially ambitious. Yet he consistently dated women who wanted to push their values onto him. Fred would respond passively while, underneath, his resentment grew. When he was moody or depressed, these women would try to get him to "snap out of it." Fred would respond by further withdrawal and, if pushed too far, would become explosive. Eventually either he would feel too hemmed in by the woman's demands, or she would feel too frustrated by his moodiness and depression, and the relationship would end.

By the time he met Nancy he had become reasonably

open and accepting of his moodiness and depression. At first Nancy felt that it was her fault when Fred was in one of his moods; then she gradually realized that this was simply one part of Fred, and she felt no need to interfere.

"I feel sad when I know you're depressed or unhappy. I understand that this is something that you need to work through by yourself," was Nancy's way of relating to Fred's moodiness. During these times their contact was only perfunctory. Nancy, having sufficient inner resources of her own, and enjoying sufficient intimacy with herself, was able to wait for Fred to reach out to her again without resenting him when he was withdrawn.

Fred had never known a relationship like this. He had never felt so totally accepted by any woman. About a year after they met, they were married.

The commitment of any Intimacy of Two does not mean taking on some ponderous burden. Rather, real intimacy between two people generates its own power, its own sustenance, and becomes in itself a source of growth and nourishment for each person. When this fails to evolve it suggests a lack of real intimacy.

The creative power of an Intimacy of Two provides a foundation for new freedom, stability and growth, in ways not possible without this kind of relating.

17

NOW IS ALWAYS THE BEGINNING

Despite our best intentions and hopes, none of us can guarantee that an intimate relationship will endure for the rest of our lives. Even formal marriage vows are at best only a declaration of intent. They simply represent the fantasy that through promises and contracts we can control our future. We want to assure ourselves and our Intimate Other that our feelings will always be as they are now.

The desire for permanence in an Intimacy of Two is expressed more realistically in the attitudes and ways two people relate with each other. The feeling of commitment which is part of the essence of a two-people intimacy can become increasingly intense and stable but can never be taken for granted.

Intimate relationships may become obsolete for countless reasons—both nourishing and toxic. When this happens, the nourishing person faces this reality and is open about it with his Intimate Other.

There is no way to whitewash the sadness of a deteriorating intimacy.

Being open and honest under the circumstances of an obsolete relationship is almost invariably a very difficult undertaking. Two people who have had an intimate relationship of some duration have meshed their lives together in many ways. Their mutual dependency and patterns of sharing represent a great deal of meaningful experience. The letting go, the rejection by one person of his previously Intimate Other, is part of the sadness—part of the pain—of living.

I've Been Had

Awareness, growth and maturity do not mean that we can no longer be manipulated or poisoned by others or that any of us are ever immune to toxic relating. Similarly, there is no way we can insure ourselves against the pain of discovering that we have made a poor choice in our selection of the person with whom we seek to create an Intimacy of Two.

When we discover that our relating lacks, or has lost, the intimate qualities we need, we may further poison ourselves by attempting to push the whole unpleasant business out of our awareness in order to avoid the pain of confronting ourselves with the reality. We hope that somehow the difficulties will go away. Or we poison ourselves by giving in to our embarrassment and even avoid revealing our concern or anxiety to the other person. Sometimes we are so fearful that people will gossip, ridicule or even delight in our difficulties that we maintain a false front and continue to live as if our relationship were truly intimate and gratifying.

One of the most lethal ways of poisoning ourselves is to swallow our integrity and self-respect in order to look good and maintain an acceptable social façade in the eyes of those around us.

This kind of toxic resignation poisons our present and future potential for discovering new intimacy either with the person we are currently involved with or someone else.

The end of an Intimacy of Two against our will is similar to a loss through death. Rationalizing, explaining or blaming oneself or the other is nothing but an exercise in futility. Pondering what we might have done and regretting what we didn't do are only ways of adding to our pain and poisoning ourselves even more. At such times we may feel that we will never get over our loss or that there will never be another person with whom we will enjoy such deep, rich, intimate relating. The pain and sadness of rejecting or losing make it difficult to feel any real comfort or solace even when our intellect or well-meaning people assure us that "this too shall pass."

I Won't Accept What Is

MARY: I don't want to see you any more. I don't feel our relationship is going anyplace. We've been fighting more and more lately.

JOHN: But I love you. We can work these things out. You're not giving it a chance.

MARY: That's what you keep telling me, that things will be different, and all these months I feel things have been getting worse.

JOHN: I just can't end it this way. I can't stand not seeing you any more. I need you.

MARY: I expect to be lonely, too. And there are other people in the world.

JOHN (*teary-eyed*): There's no one like you. I don't want to give you up. I won't give you up.

MARY: John, I'm finished. It's all over.

JOHN: I'm getting too upset. I'm going now and I'll call you later.

MARY: Please don't call. I don't want to hear from you.
   (*John leaves.*)
   (*Mary is home alone that evening and the phone rings.*)

MARY: Hello.

JOHN: Hi! It's me. I hope you've changed your mind by now.

MARY: No, I haven't, and I asked you not to call.

JOHN: I can't let go of you like this. There must be some way we can work it out.

MARY: We're just repeating the same thing over and over. There are just too many things in our relationship that I don't like. (*Conversation continues, rehashing old grievances for the next twenty minutes.*)

MARY: John, I want to hang up.

JOHN: I'll call you again tomorrow.

MARY: I don't want to hear from you. I want to make a clean break of it.

JOHN: I love you so much, I don't know what I'll do without you.

MARY: I'm going to hang up now.
   (*Mary hangs up.*)

> (*The following night Mary is home and has company.
> The phone rings.*)
>
> MARY: Hello.
>
> JOHN: I love you, Mary. Please talk to me.
>
> MARY: I'm busy. I have some people over.
>
> JOHN: Just talk to me for a few minutes. When can I see you?
>
> MARY: I don't want to see you. I've told you that—
>
> (*In the next three or four weeks there are further episodes in which John calls or unexpectedly shows up at Mary's apartment. Their conversations are essentially repetitions of the above.*)

The need to go through the pain of a mourning period for the loss of an Intimacy of Two is not essentially much different from mourning a loss through death. Often it is a *more* difficult mourning ("Maybe my Intimate Other will reconsider"). Rather than wallowing, which is a self-poisoning game, N people mourn as the most expedient way of letting go of their lost relationship, so that they are again available for new intimacies and living in the now.

Instead of finishing the mourning process, T people often short-circuit their mourning by embarking on a determined ("I'm going to make myself") campaign to busy themselves meeting new people and seeking new relationships before they are ready. Despite good intentions this often becomes a depressing experience.

When we are still in a mourning phase following the loss of an Intimate Other, we simply are not emotionally available for new relationships.

We cannot program ourselves so that three months or six months or nine months is time enough for mourning and then after that we "should" stop mourning. The mourning period within each person runs its course in its own fashion, and any attempts to interrupt or short-circuit it become self-induced, toxic manipulation. Mourning is a part of the spontaneous flow of the self. The best we can do is not disrupt it but accept it as a process in which our evolving self is assimilating an experience of loss. Most methods used to hasten the mourning period result in repression, pushing out of awareness the unfinished need to mourn. A continuing depression and feeling of futility or despair are often a body statement of unfinished mourning and a refusal to let go of the past, of what was and is no more. Only the mourner can tell when the mourning period is ending and when he or she is beginning to be emotionally available for new intimacies. Even then it is usually unrealistic to expect to be eager to meet new people. N people do not expect new relationships to make them forget the loss of an old intimacy.

Toxic people become discouraged when they find that each new person does not fill the shoes of the one for whom they mourn.

For N people each day *is* the first day of the rest of their lives. Regardless of past "failures" or other excuses, they move toward new intimacy with others. They live in the now. They seek relationships that are nourishing in the now and that offer a potential for a new Intimacy of Two. Doing the best they can to create new intimate relationships reflects their self-nourishing attitude of continuous functioning in their quest to satisfy their needs. They allow themselves no excuses for wallowing in despair. They know that the world is full of nourishing people who are searching for the same thing—the same kind of intimate relating which they themselves have experienced in the past and seek again for the now and the future.

Beyond Intimacy

When we become aware and fully appreciate the vast range of human experiences available to each of us, it becomes more natural (and easier) to accept the limitations of *any* specific relationship. Being obsessed with attaining intimate relationships implies that awareness of our full range of potentials has not yet emerged.

In our quest for a fuller, more complete self and a meaningful life-style, all relating including an Intimacy of Two remains only one aspect of the totality of our needs.

The aware person, whose potentials have ripened, is intensely involved in many aspects of living and is generally more enthusiastic, more alive. He has found a more balanced responsiveness to his various needs. He functions in a flowing, harmonious fashion as he turns his attention from one need to another on the basis of an awareness and inner directedness toward what is most important to him as his life unfolds day by day—even moment by moment.

There is no realistic way to escape the responsibility of continually choosing between various needs. When we reach out for one thing, at that instant we give up something else.

Lorraine grew up in a home where her integrity as a person was recognized from the moment she was born. Within the family, there existed a quality of glowing warmth in which she, her parents and her brother and sister all seemed to thrive. Lorraine's parents had strong values and beliefs and were openly committed to them. They were equally open in giving their reasons when they opposed some of their children's desires.

Lorraine enjoyed experimenting with new activities and interests. Although she had many interests, her love for music dated back to her earliest memories. She loved to spend hours at the piano either playing or creating short compositions. Her work as a computer programmer was stimulating and challenging. In four years she had advanced several steps within the company. She had several close girl friends with whom she felt a kind of relatedness different from that she felt with her family or with men.

She wanted children. She was also aware how important her profession, her music and her friendships were. Her busy life-style required continual compromise, which she insisted on determining for herself. Before she met Arnie, she had been deeply involved with Frank, and they had planned to marry. She broke their engagement when Frank began demanding that she spend more of her time with him. In the past, when she was involved with a man, she would gradually give up more and more of her other interests. By the time she met Arnie she was aware that, while her need for intimacy was essential, other needs were also important, and she was no longer willing to give them up.

This was one of the nourishing aspects of their relationship, since Arnie also had a growing interest in a variety of activities. He had divorced his wife after a short marriage, primarily because she had insisted on what he felt was excessive "togetherness." Her clinging attitude became more and more suffocating. After his divorce he had resolved to avoid relationships with anyone not interested in independent activities and separate friends of her own.

Lorraine and Arnie exemplify the kind of intimacy that places all relationships in the realistic perspective of being only a part, however essential, of one's total needs.

Conclusion

If all our needs were satisfied, there would be no reason for us to experiment or seek to discover new ways of relating to others and to the world. Only when we feel enough frustration and pain are we sufficiently motivated to make the effort and take the risks of discovering and experimenting with new, less-frustrating ways of satisfying our needs. This is part of human growth, and the pain of growth is the psychic pain of the anxiety, tension and catastrophic expectations we experience when we take the risk of reaching out to discover new, more gratifying ways of getting what we want.

Similarly, none of us can learn how to sustain an Intimacy of Two without the pain of frustrating experiences and various toxic encounters and relationships. An inevitable aspect of discovering what we want in our relationships is discovering what we don't want.

Experimenting with life and learning by assimilating our experiences *is* the growth process of the nourishing self. This is the most exciting, the most vigorous attitude we can adopt in our search for a philosophy and life-style, a search in which *we* discover through our *own* experiences what suits us best. It means that all our experiences, both nourishing and toxic, provide us with greater awareness of the reality of ourselves, others and our world. Any experience, even the most toxic, has the potential for enhancing our ability to continue to discover a nourishing life-style through creative adjustment. This is the glowing possibility that is always present. Despite the joys and sorrows, the fulfillments and tragedies of our lives prior to this very moment, the possibility of newly emerging excitement and meaningful experiencing is endless. Establishing and sustaining an Intimacy of Two is a natural evolution of basic human emotions and human needs.

Too often in our quest for an Intimate Other we detour ourselves by clinging to numerous relationships that we know lack real and enduring intimacy. The despair that so many feel, often through most of their lives, over the possibility of never sharing an Intimacy of Two is primarily a reflection of the toxic patterns with which we relate to others, or a reflection of their toxic patterns to which we, knowingly or not, subject ourselves. Yet the potential for greater awareness and for discovering more nourishing ways of relating to ourselves and to others continues throughout our lives.

When we are aware that a one-to-one relationship is what we want and when there is a mutual feeling of commitment between ourselves and another person, sustaining an Intimacy of Two is not a spectacular achievement. Rather, it is the spontaneous growth that springs from relating to each other.

More than any other kind of relationship, an Intimacy of Two generates its own cohesiveness and stability. It is an ongoing source of nourishment and expanding horizons. As a source of strength to sustain us against the adversities and frustrations of life, it is second only to the inner strength that comes from intimacy with ourselves.

Good contact with our Intimate Self and our Intimate Other provides enormous energy with which to relate to our world in a most satisfying, most meaningful and creative fashion. It provides us with the ability to experience great joy and excitement because of the limitless potential for self-discovery and growth and the increasing ability to function in the world. This is the optimal condition for fulfillment of our self and for living a meaningful, nourishing life.